What people are saying

Dr Talat Azad profiles six accomplished women wh makes them genuinely ins allow their significant inju  them from achieving their goals. They tell their stories in their own voices, offering an intimate glimpse of life in Pakistan where few buildings are wheelchair accessible, polio is endemic and, as one woman said, *"this baseless belief that my physical condition is a punishment from God, was ruthlessly shared."*

Universal themes emerge from these women's stories, including the importance of family and friends, never giving up, and advocacy. I was left with a heightened awareness of the struggles these women faced...and I have tremendous respect for them and all that they have achieved.

Susan Viets
Author, "Picnic at the Iron Curtain: From the Fall of the Berlin Wall to Ukraine's Orange Revolution"
susanviets.com

Wow what a collection of inspirational stories. The challenges faced by each of the protagonists in their respective struggles is difficult to fathom unless you lived it day to day.

Whether the tragedy occurred in later life or was apparent from childhood the never give up attitude of each of the ladies in this book is up-lifting. The human spirits ability to be able to overcome not just the physical disability the emotional instability and the daily struggle of life is awe inspiring. Each of these stories deserves an entire book written in more detail and perhaps a screen play devoted to the main characters.

Ishtaq Mohammed
Dentist NHS, UK

'I was written off!! Stories of inner strength and determination' keeps you engrossed while delivering an inspiring message to an audience. The author does an amazing job by combing the aspirations and dreams of six talented women into short real-life stories on their achievements despite their struggles of being differently abled in Pakistan. It is an inspiring and optimistic book which gives one hope even when things do not seem hopeful.

Dr Saima Rauf
Consultant Gynaecologist, UK

Dr Azad writes with clarity and compassion. The powerful thought-provoking narrations have confirmed many layers of stigma, discrimination in our business and social environs. In this post-truth era such authentic accounts are much needed."

Dr.Rakhshinda Perveen
Gender equality and social inclusion expert

The amazing thing about the stories in this book is that they are from the heart and make us (able people) see the world from a new perspective. Each story shows the support network each woman received and the encouragement they had in helping them achieve and become the women they are today. I am impressed by their wisdom, progressiveness and boldness.

Zohra Nisar Hunzai
Social & Behaviour Change Specialist | SBC Section
UNICEF

One of my favourite parts of the book was reading the role the parents, siblings and friends played in the life of each individual. When we think of disability, we usually only think of the sole individual affected, not the loved ones who support that person in the darkest of nights and the brightest of days. Their sacrifices, trials and efforts bring to light the true effect of a differently abled life.

Dr Samia Adil
Department of Sexual & Reproductive Health
Psychosexual & Relationship Therapist Lewisham and Greenwich NHS Trust

About the author

Born in Pakistan and educated in Pakistan and the United Kingdom, Dr Talat Azad completed her doctorate in education research at Kings College London. She is a citizen of two cultures and has worked in these two countries, which has helped shape her vision and perspectives. Starting her career in special education and moving into mainstream and inclusive education, the last three decades of Dr Talat's life have been spent advocating the rights of the disabled, equality and inclusion, women empowerment, early intervention, and early childhood education.

I was written off is her first book, based on the real-life stories of seven courageous women who, against all odds, have battled through and succeeded in their chosen profession.

Dr Talat Azad lives in London along with her husband.

Acknowledgements

I couldn't have started writing this book or even put my ideas to paper if it wasn't for some very important people. Mukarram, my dear husband, was the first who encouraged me and raised the bar high, changing the idea of a single article about one story into a whole book. Dr Jane Jones was also instrumental in endorsing my work and writing the foreword, and my dear friend, Fauzia Khuhro, introduced me to Chris Day from Filament publishing, who took an immediate interest in the idea of my book.

I am also thankful to Sadia Atta, Lubna Muzzammil, Mona Adeel and Dr Mukhtar Ahmed, who helped me find the six amazing women I write about. Munazzah Anwar encouraged me all the way, and I thank all my family and friends for their unstinting belief and faith in me.

I'm a queen of procrastination and knowing my weakness, if it wasn't for Chris Day my publisher and Roy Francis, my editor, both now good friends, this book would never have seen the light of day; big thanks to you both!!

Huge thanks also to you, Zarina Hasan for the beautiful artwork you have created for this book and Dania Khan; you have done magic with the graphic design.

I also want to acknowledge all my reviewers who took time out from their busy schedules and gave very valuable feedback and reviews. There are numerous more names of friends, colleagues and family who have been there for me when I much needed them; THANK YOU ALL!

As would be expected I have made every effort to be as accurate as I can, and therefore any omissions and errors in this book are my own

Dedication

This book is dedicated to my ever-loving parents who I owe everything to what I am today...

And to all the brave and courageous women out there who have battled and achieved against all odds and have been the agents of change!!!

Published by
Filament Publishing Ltd
14, Croydon Road, Beddington
Croydon, Surrey CR0 4PA UK
+44(0)20 8688 2598
www.filamentpublishing.com

© 2022 Dr Talat Azad

ISBN 978-1-913623-49-4

All the proceeds of the book sale will go to Indus Hospital
and Health Network (IHHN) UK
https://indushospital.org.uk/.

"I was written off!!"

Six true-life stories of inner
strength and determination

by

Dr Talat Azad

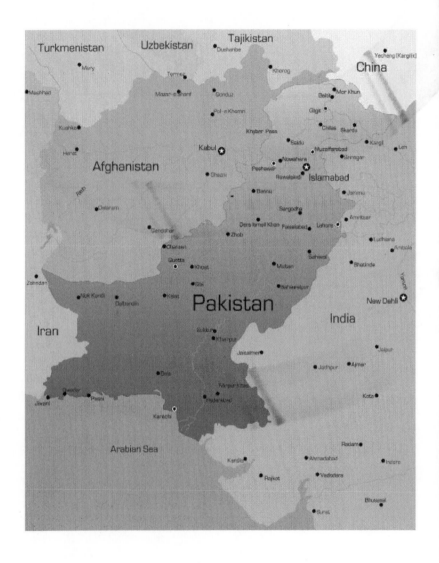

Table of Contents

Reviews   1

About the Author   4

Acknowledgements   5

Map of Pakistan   10

Foreword   13

Introduction   16

Anam's story   19

Hina's story   49

Nuzhat 's story   73

Tanzila's story   93

Uzma's story   115

Zarina's story   145

Foreword

D r Talat's works in the field of special, inclusive and mainstream education define her whole personality. Since I have known her, she has been a true advocate for people with disabilities. Being an educationist, she is a true activist, and for nearly three decades, Dr Talat has been propagating and working on disability rights, inclusive education, women empowerment, early intervention, and early childhood education.

This is Dr Talat's first non-academic work since her doctorate, in which she shares with us the life stories of, Anam consultant psychiatrist, activist, soft skills trainer and motivational speaker; Hina dental surgeon and motivational speaker; Nuzhat business entrepreneur; Tanzila business entrepreneur, activist and writer; Uzma human resource specialist, social worker and certified success coach and Zarina doctor, virologist, artist and motivational speaker.

These human stories of courage and determination present themselves to us every day, but do we really think about them? Does it have an impact on us? Does it move us? Writing these real-life stories of courage and determination, Dr Talat wants these stories to be heard, want able bodies to take note, and hopes that the courage and determination of the women she writes about will lead to long overdue changes in the lives of the disabled.

The stories in this collection from six brave women from Pakistan with varying disabilities, provide accounts of their experiences that are at the same time harrowing yet giving hope. No 'fluffy' language or sentimental or sanitized accounts, the stories reveal the realities and indignities of these women's physical disablement as well as the mental stresses. Entirely lacking in self- pity, although this does not mean to say that the women do not at times suffer depression or some bouts of despair, the seven case studies show these women picking up the pieces in the light of their disablement to re-purpose their lives differently rather than succumbing to self- pity and the challenge of questionable attitudes from 'outsiders'.

They are fortunate to have supportive families and friends – and not everyone does- but the greatest strength comes from each individual's determination and acute sense of self- worth, refusing to be defined by their disability. Their beliefs are a source of comfort and support. Developing a 'can do' attitude is crucial but this can only be done in a culture of practical and inclusive support for all, whatever the disability, a culture that shows empathy and seeks practical solutions, not just empty pitying rhetoric.

The challenges for these women are enormous, often generated by the views and perceptions of able others in the community and society at large, but also in confronting the physical challenges they have to face in the light of considerable lack of equal opportunities to construct and live their lives. The women provide a counter- challenge and drawing on their faith, demonstrate a powerful mindset and absolute determination to speak out, aim high and refuse to be 'written off'. On the contrary, they write themselves into new broader narratives of inclusivity and turn their attention, inspiringly, to helping others.

The stories provide an opportunity to explore in depth the women's disabilities through their lens and invite the reader to reflect as 'outsider' as to how a deeper understanding might be reached in order to engage as constructively as possible in promoting and enacting inclusivity.

Dr Jane Jones
Senior Lecturer in Education
King's College London

Introduction

I was written off!

Stories of inner strength and determination

*S*ajawat (adornment) was my mother's labour of love. It produced hand embroideries, handmade paintings, home linens, dresses, outfits, and accessories. *Sajawat* in Pakistan was unique in providing employment for women artisans and workers. It kept me engaged and took care of my creative side, which I think I inherited from my parents. *Sajawat* was a hobby, and although it was satisfying and inspiring, I felt that I still needed to do something more worthwhile with my life.

Destiny would have it that one day I saw an advertisement in my local newspaper about Anjuman e Behbood e Samat e Atfal – ABSA school for the deaf, who was hiring staff. Out of interest, I called them and was invited to visit the school. My life took a three-sixty-degree turn when I entered ABSA school that fine morning in 1990. There was so much laughter and joy; both the school and students caught my attention and interest and won my heart. From there on, my outlook on life completely changed. That experience has influenced my education and career and has shaped and moulded me into what I am today. That was nearly three decades ago, and I have never looked back.

Today I work in mainstream and inclusive education, which has brought me much joy and a sense of worth. It has taught me gratitude, patience, resilience, and profound respect for those with disabilities. I have also been privileged to have met hundreds of children and adults with disabilities. They have impacted my life and led me to a deeper understanding of the issues of disability and the rights of the disabled.

In 2019, just before the world-wide covid epidemic, I met Nuzhat Abbas, whose story I write about in this book. She was visiting from Lahore in Pakistan, and it was fascinating to watch her in her wheelchair navigating the streets and London transport so joyfully. Despite contracting polio as a child, Nuzhat's positive attitude and zest for life intrigued me. I wanted to know more about her, more about her life, achievements, and struggles. This led me to write her story and the stories of five other remarkable women like her from Pakistan. They are Dr. Anam Najam, a consultant psychiatrist and motivational speaker from Muzaffarabad, Azad Kashmir, Pakistan; Dr. Hina Sheikh, a dental surgeon and motivational speaker from Karachi; Ms. Tanzila Khan, a business entrepreneur, activist and writer from Lahore; Ms. Uzma Shah, a human resource executive, certified success coach and motivational speaker from Karachi; and Dr. Zarina Hasan, a doctor, virologist, activist, artist and motivational speaker from Islamabad.

Throughout our meetings, interviews, and discussions, I felt a powerful positivity about these women. There were no complaints, cribbing, or resentment as they shared their deepest thoughts and feelings with me. They opened their homes, hearts, and inner souls, and I've tried to show a glimpse of their lives as people with disabilities. Hopefully, I also show how with the help and support of their families, they have been able to overcome their disabilities. These are inspirational women, and their lives and journeys have brought to the fore, the problems and challenges that people with disabilities face in Pakistan every day.

Overcoming their disabilities, the women I write about in this book are an example and have helped raise awareness of the disabled in Pakistan. They are examples of the resourcefulness of the human spirit and what can be achieved with resolve and determination. They inspire, shine and are a force to be reckoned with. I am passionate about them and their stories; telling us all not to give up but to push through, despite our circumstances. They are my role model; nothing can or will stop them. They inspire me, and I know they will inspire others, not least people with disabilities. They have put their trust in me, and I hope I have been faithful in telling their stories. I trust I have done them justice; for one thing, it is clear that their journey continues!!

Anam's story

I used to be fed up with the pain, but I never questioned Him about the disability; the only request was to stop the pain. In fact, it made me realise that I was blessed with a healthy and able mind and body for twenty-one years. I never thanked Allah for these countless blessings. So, I felt I had no right to complain, at least for the next twenty-one years!!!

I belong to the beautiful valley of Azad Jammu and Kashmir (AJK), a nominally self-governing territory administered by Pakistan that is part of the western portion of the larger Kashmir region. Kashmir has been the subject of a dispute between India and Pakistan since 1947. It has a population of nearly five million people and its capital, Muzaffarabad, is a fertile, green mountainous beautiful, landscaped valley, where I was born and brought up.

My parents and I lived with my grandparents in Muzaffarabad with one elder and younger brother. I was blessed to be born in this beautiful area, and as a child, I was told that I was very mischievous but never bothered my parents. Naughty but well behaved and strong in academic work. I was six years old when I completed the recitation of the Holy Quran, and besides my academic subjects, I would fully participate in the extracurricular activities of my school, so I guess you could take mischief as a sign of intellect!

My love of books and poetry comes from my grandparents. My Dada (my paternal grandfather) was interested in poetry, and so was I. He was fond of Allama Iqbal's poetry, and I learnt some of his poetry by heart. Iqbal is the national poet of Pakistan and I got attracted to his poetry because there is wisdom in it. Even at a young age, I could relate to his poetry and its broad vision. I went into clinical depression when my Dadi (paternal grandmother) died, and it took me six months to recover from this trauma. However, my studies were going well, and I was a position holder in matriculation. A matriculation certificate is issued to one who has cleared 10th grade in school in Pakistan.

It was a beautiful winter's day. My older brother and I were at home, my younger brother at school and my parents and grandfather out on different errands. I was on vacation from college and was eighteen years old at that time. I was in my room when I suddenly felt everything shaking and crumbling down. I got up from my bed and started to run; I got to the lounge, and walls were collapsing around me, the floor was moving, I fell, and everything fell on top of me. I could not understand anything. I was bleeding, and there was darkness everywhere because rubble was around me from the whole house, but I was still conscious. It took a while, and when I was able to gain my senses, I saw some light coming in from one side. Still, there wasn't enough space for me to sit up, I was lying on the rubble, so I got all my energy and crawled towards the light. I started to recite the kalima (the formal content of the shahada declaration of faith in Islam) - "There is no God but Allah, and Muhammad is the messenger of Allah". Thinking this was the end... what is ahead? Death? Accountability? I was reading the kalima; I have read that whoever is blessed to recite the kalima before death, will be blessed, and Allah (the one and only God in Islam) will forgive all their sins.

With this thought, I started to crawl towards that light and finally managed to get out of the wreckage with a few injuries. It was horrifying as the whole locality was rubble but what kept me going was the recitation of the kalima. I kept reading it aloud, and it gave me the energy to fight my way through the ruins. My first thought was to save my brother, and I started to walk amongst the debris to where his room was. All I could see was his head as the rest of his body was covered in debris and huge stones as our house was built of big rocks. I kept reciting the kalima and kept thinking about how I could move such heavy stones; honestly, it was due to reciting the kalima, that I felt strong enough and finally got my brother out.

All we could hear were people screaming and crying around us; many were buried under the rubble. We were injured, bleeding...our clothes were torn... the two of us had no knowledge how and where were the rest of the family was? Abbu (my father) finally was able to reach us; he also had a head injury and could not remember where he was and what had happened. Ammi (my mother) was buried for five hours in the ruins of my Nani's (maternal grandmother) house before anyone was able to get her out. As a result, she was unable to walk for many hours.

This is how the famous earthquake that hit Kashmir and some northern areas of Pakistan on the 8th of October 2005 affected my family. In Kashmir, the three central districts were badly affected. Muzaffarabad (my home city) and the state capital were the hardest hit. Hospitals, schools, and rescue services were paralysed, including the police and the armed forces. There was virtually no infrastructure, and communication was severely affected. More than 70% of all casualties were estimated to have occurred in Muzaffarabad. Moreover, it was October, and we were already into the winter weather. Nearly 100,000 precious lives were lost; sadly, I lost my precious Dada and my Nani and two of my cousins!

That night we were without any roof... out in the open in a park, injured and hungry with nothing to eat... there was the rain, storm, and heavy winds like tornados and aftershocks from the earthquake. How the earth was moving, it seemed nobody would be saved from this ordeal. The rain was not stopping, and there was nothing above to cover us. Someone had cooked some rice and had brought it in a big bag, and everyone took a handful of it to keep going. You know how ironic it is, and how careful we are about hygiene, but at that time, we were all sorts of people and putting our hands in the bag and eating from it. It seemed such a blessing that handful of rice!!!... It was such a strange and horrifying situation with so many people...when one had to use the toilet, you would go and urinate in the bushes. Still, as my mother was unable to walk, she had to crawl to relieve herself!

There was nothing left after the earthquake...all the roads were closed, and there were landslides, which meant no vehicle could reach us. Hospitals had collapsed, people were stuck, and everything was finished. The next morning some people had started to walk on foot, and some people did manage to bring help, after which helicopters began arriving. I remember the next morning we buried our Dada after we found his body. There were no funeral prayers, no shrouding with the special cloth, as per the Islamic faith. We thought that the body should be buried as soon as possible, because in such a situation, we feared that the longer the body remains unburied, this may cause putrefaction. We dug our Dada's grave and buried him ourselves.

Our family took the only land route open to us to Lahore, which was via Abbottabad, where we stayed with my father's sister. Only emergency cases were being airlifted.

It was a very traumatic event … we had no money, everything was gone!!!

We stayed in Lahore for a few days and then went back to Muzaffarabad. Our house was destroyed, but we had another home in the city, which was rented out.

Since we were bound by contract, we could not ask the tenants to vacate. So, they were inside, and we put up a tent outside and started living there. We lived like this for nearly a month. I remember somebody had provided us with mattresses, and since these were very thin, we could feel the pricking of some wheat corns which must have been planted in the past. There were hardly any buildings left… everyone was living in tents as we felt safer this way. We all feared going into a building or house, because we thought it would collapse because of the aftershocks.

Those two post-earthquake months were very traumatic, and I heaved a sigh of relief when I was admitted to Ayub Medical College, Abbottabad. It was a big escape for me from this distressing situation and I was relieved when I left to go to do my medical studies, which provided me with a very positive outlet. I took pride in my studies and enjoyed the extracurricular activities as well. It was a perfect time, and I thoroughly loved every aspect of my college life.

The third year of medical studies had started, and I was invited to go on a hiking trip as I was a club member. Even though I was an adult and did not need to ask permission, culturally, I asked my parent's permission to take this trip. Out of love for me, my mother suggested that I join them instead and go to Rawalpindi to attend a family wedding.

The idea behind this was that my mother thought I needed a break from my studies and the trip would be a good chance to meet my family. So instead of going hiking, I attended the family wedding in Rawalpindi.

After the wedding on March 15th, 2008, we planned to leave at night for the 5-hour car journey to Muzaffarabad. Night travel was preferred to avoid the traffic and the heat during the day. We were four of us, with my father driving, my uncle in the passenger front seat and my mother and I in the back. Tired from the day's events and, as a habit, sitting in the back seat, I immediately went to sleep on my mother's shoulder.

At the start of our journey, my father stopped at a petrol station to get petrol, while my mother put something in the boot. It was obvious by the car and what we had in it that we were returning from a wedding. However, my father noticed a vehicle parked at the petrol station with some people in it. He was always a fast driver and noticed that one car passed him on our way. All the inmates of that car peeped into ours when they passed us. My father found this strange, for who could drive faster than him? Within a few minutes, he turned a curve and saw a car stop in the middle of the road. One person was sitting inside, and one was outside the vehicle. They signalled for us to stop. My father slowed the car, and while he was nearing, two people came toward him with guns. Realising the situation, he sped away, and at that moment, the people with the guns opened fire.

One bullet broke the back windscreen and went through the seat and into my mother's arm causing her great pain. I was jolted from my sleep by the noise and shouting and heard my mother reciting the kalima. I couldn't understand what was happening. I thought our car brakes had failed, but my father, believing that the armed robbers were following us, drove even faster. At this point, my mother calmly said that her arm was bleeding. I could not understand why she was bleeding. *What happened?* I asked. She said, *'I have been shot at!!'*

Abbu kept asking if we were OK, and Ammi said yes as she was worried, he might stop the car, which she did not want for fear of the robbers catching up with us. Her arm was bleeding, but in the darkness, we could not see that blood was also coming from my neck. I did have a strange sensation at the back of my neck and tried to move my arm, but I could not!! I asked my uncle to help me sit up straight, but even he didn't know the extent of my injury. About 10- 15 minutes passed before Abbu realised we were injured. He stopped and asked for help and was guided to a nearby dispensary.

We managed to get to the dispensary, where the medical staff treated my mother, bandaged her arm, and gave us the good news that the bullet had left her body and her wound was superficial. My parents wanted me to be checked out, as I was complaining about some pain. When I tried to get out of the car, I couldn't move to open the door nor able to move my leg. My parents thought I was scared and in shock because of the incident. Eventually, my father lifted me and took me inside the dispensary.

The medical staff examining me said, *"the bullet is still in her neck, and there is no exit wound!!!"*. They told my parents to rush me to a hospital. Slowly it dawned on us, what had happened!!! My father and uncle then settled me back in the car's front passenger seat, and we set off to a hospital. We didn't think of immobilising my neck as my injury was spinal. However, I remember telling my uncle that he should hold me from my back, especially my neck, as I was swaying and falling and couldn't maintain my balance.

We reached Muzaffarabad hospital, and after some initial tests, it was confirmed that a bullet was trapped behind my neck in the spinal cord, so it was a neurosurgery case. Muzaffarabad hospital did not have this facility, so we were advised to go to Rawalpindi Hospital. The hospital inserted a urine catheter, and there was no movement in my legs and arms. There was so much pain that even the airwaves around me would cause me so much distress that I would scream with the pain. However, as advised, we set off for Pakistan Institute of Medical Sciences (PIMS), Islamabad, in an ambulance the hospital provided.

The doctors removed the bullet at PIMS, Islamabad. My mind was numb and unable to process the accident and the implications this would have for my future. I remember I was so much in denial and casual about what had happened. It had not sunk in. Even talking to my friends on the phone, I lightly described what had happened. After my operation, I even asked my uncle to preserve the bullet so I could keep it and use it in my medical forensic notebook as a case history.

Unfortunately, in Pakistan, there is still no culture of talking to the patient and updating on the facts and scenarios of a medical condition. So not surprisingly, the doctors shared the prognosis of my condition with my family and not with me. This was 2008, and I was a third-year medical student by now and 21 years old! On my enquiry every morning during the medical rounds, the doctors would keep soothing me with the answer to keep praying as they were doing the same. All I knew was that I had a spinal cord injury. I later learned that my condition is quadriplegia, and I had become a quadriplegic. In this condition, the body is paralysed from at least the shoulders down. Paralysis results from damage to the spinal cord, which prevents messages from the brain from being able to be sent to the rest of the body. Sometimes I would be pacified that I would be able to walk in 6 months, which I later realised had no truth.

I was in hospital for one and a half months. It was not just a very hard time for me but also for my family, especially my mother, as she also had to take care of her injury. During my hospital stay, my condition was bad. I used to develop all kinds of infections, my blood pressure would drop low, and I would often need oxygen. We could not understand what was happening, and my parents were told clearly that I would be in this condition for life and that they should not expect any improvement.

We were not given any information about long-term rehabilitation, advice, suggestions, further treatment, therapies...no, nothing!!

Amidst all this, the kind of support I got from my family and friends was unimaginable. They made all kinds of sacrifices and provisions to help and see me through this difficult time. I considered myself very lucky to be on the receiving end of this love and affection. Friends would bring news about college happenings, and I would feel *"I'm missing out on so much"*. During my hospital stay, I requested my course books from home. I was not allowed to sit as they had immobilised my neck, so I would raise my head, put my books on the pillow, and study. I could not turn the page without mobility in my arms, and my mother would do so for me.

Realisation struck when I came home and faced a mirage of physical and psychological issues. These problems I understood much later came with becoming a quadriplegic overnight. I would have so much pain in my hands that I would need someone all the time to blow on them; it was as if they were burning. This condition was because of the nerve damage in my hands, and nerves never heal or regenerate. Medicines at this point were proving ineffective, and every day was a struggle.

Our religion and culture have a strong sense of hospitality, but this generosity is often abused. Relatives, family, friends, neighbours etc., were always visiting me; they would expect to be fed and looked after. So, it was burdensome for my family; they had to look after me, there was a lack of sleep as they had to give day and night duties for me and on top of that visitors... and they would be there for long hours...it was too much!! Not just their presence, but their negative behaviour and remarks of pity caused my family and me much distress. This baseless belief that my physical condition was a punishment from God was ruthlessly shared, regardless of its effect on my family and me. On our end, we were helpless and could not ask such people to leave for fear of broken kinship ties.

I also underwent severe depression; there was so much anger and despair in me... that it was difficult for me to think clearly...I had started cursing ... *"may this happen to everyone what has happened to me. Especially who did this to me, he should have it. I wish I could get hold of that person, and I want to put him through the same ordeal and then ask him how you feel? Ask his family how they feel? He does not even know what he has done, shot us randomly, or even know what happened to me"*. The worst part was that I was lashing out this anger at my loved ones, especially at Ammi, as she was in my direct line of fire. I would start doubting her every action towards me, e.g., food that she fed me, *"I will not eat this, you all want me to die"*.

I had sleepless nights because of the nerve pain in my hands... facing another day with the same issues and fearing another sleepless night was just too much to endure. Then, when I was in pain, my mother would read several prayers and some of them she put up near my bedside. I would pray, but at times when I was in a lot of pain, I would have a conversation with Allah Almighty, *"Allah, I have to ask you, and sadly there is no one else I can ask so, please relieve me of this pain as only you can do it".'*

Then I would have these conversations very loudly, *"please stop this pain...I can't take this anymore...just stop this, please!".*

I used to be fed up with the pain, but I never questioned Him about the disability; the only request was to stop the pain. In fact, it made me realise that I was blessed with a healthy and able mind and body for twenty-one years. I never thanked Allah for these countless blessings. So, I felt I had no right to complain, at least for the next twenty-one years!!!

Since I was a kid, I have always felt a spiritual connection with Allah. Whenever I was in despair or wanted to thank him, I would do so in prostration. I remember during my matriculation exams, we were supposed to write an essay on *'best friend',* and I wrote that my best friend is Allah. So, when this accident happened, I used to be in pain, asking him to relieve me of it; the thought that Allah tests his special chosen people always used to be at the back of my mind.

It's hard to believe, but before this accident, I shared with my roommate that *"sometimes people have headaches, fever etc... but nothing happens to me. Why? It is said that people Allah loves he sends calamities and tests them with hardships...but Allah doesn't send any* hardships my way, that means he doesn't like me or finds me so bad?".

Strangely after this, I had my accident. The thought stayed with me that I had asked for this myself. On top of it I say that he is my best friend!!...so if you are his friend, then his friends must be worthy of his love, and they are the ones who face the maximum number of tests and hardships. During my pain, I would tell Allah, *"I am not worthy of your friendship. I was terribly mistaken…. I am a mortal human being; please let me be like that; forgive me; it was my mistake. I am not at all worthy of your friendship…I'm sorry, I'm done here. I can't do it… I cannot afford friendship with you!!".*

After the shock of the accident had settled in, there was a discussion about continuing with my medical studies. This was ruled out! The consensus was to do my degree in some other field. At this point, I thought to myself, *"no, this is wrong"* and I kept asking myself, *"why should I leave my studies? If I cannot walk, what does it have to do with my studies if my hands do not work? My brain is working; I can think, read, talk, understand, and then why?".*

I became severely depressed, lost my appetite and sleep, and became anti-social. Negativity had completely set in, and there was so much anger that I thought everyone around me was against me. They were, however, all trying to help. Obviously, my parents were also disturbed by this behaviour and wanted some respite for themselves and me. They invited our family friend, a psychiatrist, over for a meal. I still remember after days of not eating properly, he urged me to eat, and I did manage to eat a bit with him. He started my treatment and put me on anti-depressants with regular counselling. My main objective during this time was to fully gain my senses and focus on returning to my medical studies. Gradually I was working towards bringing my family to accept this possibility. The good thing about my family was that they would not argue with me about anything. They gave me maximum support but did not understand nor knew how to manage the situation we had all been thrown into.

After the accident, I had a teacher who would visit me regularly, commuting between Abbottabad and Muzaffarabad. One day he came, and I shared my thoughts with him about continuing my medical studies and asked him to speak to my father. He was able to convince him to let me take this chance of a lifetime and continue my studies.

The lines on my hands were wiped out after the accident, but new lines developed gradually. A palmist friend offered to read my palm, and upon my enquiry about re-joining my studies, he responded that there would be a gap of 2 years. I remember that night was like a doomsday night for me. I kept thinking about 2 years gap??? I kept praying to Allah and asking him that *"if you are the one who has created my destiny and if you have written this for me, then you can change it ... Allah, you will have to change it for me"*. After praying, faith had entered me that it is going to be ok, and I should now start the procedure.

On my persistence, my college agreed to form a medical board to review my case. I got a very warm welcome from all the students on the day I appeared before the board. There was even an introductory meeting with the board to fight my case. A professor who happened to be on the board gave me immense support during the whole process. I managed to satisfy the board that my physical conditions would not be an obstacle to continuing with my studies. In contrast, I was able to convince the board that I did not have to do surgery or deliveries as I could follow other fields of medicine. I posed a hypothetical question to them. *"I know I'm not physically apt to do some of the tasks I might be asked to do, but my brain is working, so let's say I had completed my degree and then this accident happened which could happen to any one of you. Would the degree be taken away from you or me? Would our academic qualifications be snatched from us? Obviously not, then why shouldn't I be given a chance?"*. The whole discussion bore fruit, and the board agreed to give me one chance, with the condition that I should pass my 3rd year at the first attempt.

There was not much time left as we were already in August, and the exams were due in January and February. Imagine, 4-5 months of the term had been wasted. Whilst I was thankful that I had been granted this opportunity, the thoughts of how I will manage in my condition, in the hostel, in a new situation etc... were nagging all the time. The night before I was supposed to join, I was very worried, and I prayed very hard and went to sleep.

In my dream, I saw the Prophet Muhammad (peace be upon him). I was crying and praying. He comforted me. The following day I woke up and felt at peace.

We decided as a family to move to Abbottabad. We took a rented house, with my father taking a few months leave from his government job. Despite my yearly medical college fees being nominal, my medical expenses increased with the move. To cover these, my father sold a plot of land. After a while, the move didn't prove practical owing to my safety and security needs, so we decided that my mother and I would move to a hostel, and my father and brother would return to Muzaffarabad.

Going back to college after my life-changing accident proved to be a journey. The college and the hostel administration supported us in many ways. Initially, they built a ramp for me in the hostel. I also developed bladder incontinence and had to use a catheter, a tube inserted into your bladder, allowing your urine to drain freely. For passing stools, I had to use diapers, and for bathing in the washroom, I was given permission to use a special space.

My friends and other hostellers always volunteered to assist my mother in shifting me from my bed to the wheelchair. They also helped to take my wheelchair every day from the hostel to my college and take me home in the evenings. Their friendship and the cooperation made me wonder if they were humans or angels? Even fasting during Ramadan, they would still not shy away from helping. Ramadan is the ninth month of the Islamic calendar, observed by Muslims worldwide as a month of fasting, prayer, spiritual reflection, self-improvement, heightened devotion, worship and community. The fast begins at dawn and ends at sunset, so, during the hot summer months, the fasts would be 16-17 hours long. These girls still gave me unwavering support and companionship.

Keeping in mind how burdening all this must be to them, I was considering getting an electric wheelchair. However, when I shared this idea with them, they were completely against it and requested I not burden myself with this expense. College would always facilitate the classes on the ground floor; if they couldn't be arranged, the ancillary staff was always willing to lift my wheelchair up the stairs.

As part of the practical part of my course, during the rounds at the hospital, my professors would always allow me to place my wheelchair in the front. Pressure sores were the result of long hours of work and sitting on a wheelchair, but that didn't deter me from seeing this opportunity as a challenge. I had forced the college to take me in and did not feel it right to ask for special favours. At that time, I could not even sit straight in my wheelchair, so I sat in a reclined position. My teachers were aware that I used the notes prepared by my friends. As a concession, the university nominated a junior student as my scribe for examinations.

With these positive attitudes and leverages, I faced

some very negative comments. I remember a teacher telling my friends, *"You are sensible and can understand what is happening and what state she is in, so why don't you explain to your friend that she should pack up and go home"*. Another teacher said, *"what are you doing here in this condition? You should be in a rehabilitation centre"*. Then a neurosurgeon told me, *"You should be grateful you are sitting here because people in your condition do not even survive for this long"*. Yes, I should have been in rehabilitation, having my therapies to build my muscle strength and functional improvement. Still, my medical issues were so many, and I had to cope with my studies and didn't want to be left behind! This is the price I had to pay.

During the final year of my studies, we had a setback as my mother, my principal attendant and carer, was diagnosed with typhoid. It was exam time, and all my friends who had helped us throughout would also have their exams! I started my exams, but at this stage, I did not even know whether I would be able to appear in all my exams or not. A doctor friend of mine, senior to me, came to my rescue; she applied for leave from work, stayed with me for a few days, and looked after me.

Looking after me was a huge undertaking. It entailed changing my diaper, emptying my urine bag thrice a day, showering me, turning me on my side during the night, changing my clothes, feeding me, a bed to wheelchair transfer, and changing the catheter every week. To top it all, I had diarrhea and would soil myself, so my friend had to clean me and give me a shower all the time. It was too much!! One can't even imagine how much!! And think that friends can be like this...go to this extent... be so helpful!!!

We kept looking for treatment options during these years, and stem cell therapy was considered to have given positive results in some cases like mine. In stem cell therapy, they take the stem cells from your bones and inject them into your spine. The medical fraternity was divided on the outcomes of this treatment, but at that point, I was like a drowning person who needed hope. My family decided on getting the treatment in Germany. As an *Azad Jammu and Kashmir* (AJK) government employee, my father's family was also included in the medical benefits, so the government paid for my treatment abroad which cost 9000 Euros. In contrast, my father managed my living expenses, by selling a plot of land.

The process of obtaining a German visa from their embassy in Islamabad was challenging. To begin with, their shuttle service and the entire premises were not disabled friendly and did not have barrier-free access. As my wheelchair could not be taken inside the waiting area through the narrow entrance, I had to wait alone in the scorching sun. In contrast, my mother and brother were taken inside the waiting room. When the interview call came, they opened another entrance to the building. These were minor hurdles compared to the major disappointment of our visa being refused. We re-applied and had to go through the same scenario; the second time it was also rejected.

After the second refusal, I wrote to the embassy. Through correspondence, it came to light that their refusal was based on assumptions. The German government believed that I would not return to Pakistan after the completion of my treatment and would illegally remain in the country, as the quality of life for the disabled in Pakistan is not good.

Meanwhile, a television channel interviewed me, and these visa issues were highlighted in that interview. Based on this interview, there was a bit of activity on the embassy's front. On our third attempt, we were granted a visa. Still, I had to reassure the Embassy that I would return at the end of my treatment and report back to the embassy in Pakistan. I went for three weeks to get the treatment. Unfortunately, the stem cell did not help as some other complications developed. The attitude of the medical team and the hospital staff was very friendly, and the support was good.

Finally, I completed my medical studies, and the next step was to find employment. The first step in Pakistan is to register with Pakistan Medical and Dental Council (PMDC). Considering my physical limitations and based on my rehabilitation, the specialist recommendation was that I could work between three clinical fields, pathology, psychiatry, and radiology.

I had a leather strap that I used to fit in my spoon and eat. Aware of my inability to write, I thought to adjust my pen in that strap, and I started practising writing the alphabet. The first word I could write was ALLAH, but in a very crooked way.

I started my house job in psychiatry at the Combined Military Hospital (CMH), Muzaffarabad. The professor of psychiatry who I started my house job with was very cooperative. In the beginning he realised my handwriting limitations and how I was trying to cover it up. So instead of making me write the detailed case histories, he made all the proformas' of the patients, even having them photocopied at his expense and handing them to me. I take him as my mentor; he was my inspiration - he taught me to think. It was at that time I really developed an interest in psychiatry and decided to do my specialisation in this field.

In his company, I also got a chance to strengthen myself spiritually as, on his suggestion, I read the complete translation of the Holy Quran. As I mentioned earlier, I was always inclined toward poetry writing and recitation; now, I do it with the element of spirituality, and I find it very enlightening. On the other hand, a cardiology professor was also very helpful. He kept me on rotation with him for a bit in cardiology. At his request, the government gave me an electric hospital bed, followed by an electric wheelchair. It was like someone was constantly thinking about what and how things would benefit me and my needs for the future. This professor would also take up my job-related issues with the department of health and manage all of that. My family and I were entangled so much in the day-to-day affairs that we would heave a sigh of relief on the passing of each day. We were not just able to think in the long term.

After completing my house job, I applied for a position at AJK medical college. I successfully secured a position, but I was appointed to CMH Muzaffarabad in the psychiatry department, because the medical college building was not wheelchair accessible. I started my residency in psychiatry, appeared for the public service commission exam and then, as a psychiatrist, I was appointed at CMH.

At the start, when I joined the Combined Military Hospital as a full-time psychiatrist, I was on my own. After the accident, I was surrounded by friends who always helped and assisted, even when I had a manual wheelchair. A family friend who was a gynaecologist at CMH also helped me get rid of my inhibitions about going out on my own and facing the public.

My patients behaviour was positive towards me, and I sometimes felt I had an advantage because of my condition. Many of them said that they saw me as an inspiration and said that when they come to me, *"seeing you amidst all this, we forget our problems".* The psychiatric issues they have cannot be resolved by just looking at them and the stress and lack of motivation they face, are lessened they say, in seeing my problems. They feel that if she can do it, so can they! Yet occasionally, I come across offensive behaviour, where people like to make me feel as if they should get some warning from my condition, but I guess this is the whole package. I remember once my findings on a patient's medico-legal case were argued by his lawyer in court based on my disability. The judge hearing the case, refuted the claims as objectionable and baseless and, in fact, challenged him on the claims.

Most of my colleagues were very positive and supportive towards me, but at the same time, some were of the opinion that my seat should have been given to a capable able-bodied person who could have used it competently. Thankfully, such comments never caused any damage, but they kept coming. Over time I learned to counter the negative behaviour toward me by sometimes ignoring and responding in a way that was bound to impact upon the opposite person.

On the other hand, some incidences have left a deep impression on me. One day during the rush hour at the hospital, a security guard helped me by opening doors for me as I was getting late. That night in my dream I saw the same security guard at Khana e kaaba, (holy place of worship for Muslims) he was pleased, and I recognised him. So, the next day I thought I should go and tell him myself since I had such a good dream about him. I looked and looked, but I could not find him, and since that day, I have never seen him again. So, I firmly believe that he was an angel in the form of a human being sent to help me.

In the beginning, when I became a psychiatrist, it was my selfish fight for survival as I never thought this would benefit others. Gradually, when people started coming to me, and I started doing public clinics, people would come and share their experiences of how much my life have impacted on and benefitted their lives. A friend of mine thought my life story to be inspirational and requested that I come and give a talk to his students. He thought it would be good to share my life experiences with youngsters who give up on life so easily. I got an overwhelming response from the students. So, this is how motivational speaking started for me.

Initially, after these public speeches, I felt as if I had exposed everything in front of strangers, becoming naked, as if I was selling my pain. There was constant distress, which weighed very heavily on me. I did not want to discuss the happenings with family or friends; it still happens but in a milder form. Gradually I saw and felt the impact my sharing had on people facing similar dilemmas, especially parents and families who had a child with a disability and who had given up on them. This positive change has kept me going, where I can give courage to people who have lost hope.

Friends have played a vital role in my life. Even before my accident, I had always been very close and emotionally attached to two of my best friends. The accident truly made our bond stronger. The news of one of them getting married gave me immense pleasure, but also, started me thinking that I must prepare myself emotionally to deal with when both would get married and become busy in their own lives and families. It was a wake-up call. My family was there, but my social circle revolved around them. My friends and I were a very close-knit group of three. The more I thought about it, the more I felt suffocated, as I perceived life would be very difficult without them.

The thought of leaving my environment kept recurring and had me constantly thinking about my options. Of course, I could not afford to go abroad and settle down. Going abroad for higher studies started to enter my mind, making me look for scholarships to study overseas. After a few applications, I was lucky to get a Chevening scholarship. These UK Government scholarships and fellowships enable future leaders to study in the UK, whilst joining a global community of professionals who are creating positive change worldwide. I got a place on a master's programme in War and Psychiatry at the Institute of Psychiatry at King's College London.

My mother was also granted a special visa by the UK government to travel with me as my principal carer. Both the hostel and the college were very forthcoming in making all sorts of provisions to accommodate my special needs. When I went to study at King's College London through the National Health Service, I was assigned a surgery with a general practitioner, which also provided rehabilitation services to improve my own functional capabilities. Furthermore, I was given two carers who came for me both in the mornings and evenings to help in my daily living tasks. Going to the UK for my master's was one of my life's best decisions, and I owe it to divine providence.

During my stay in London, I also experienced a lot of humility from the general public and the police when I had an accident on a London bus. On this occasion, for some reason, with the bus I was getting on, the opening of the ramps to let me on, did not match the level of the bus. I had my doubts about getting on. However, I still took the risk, but as soon as I tried to get on the ramp, the front wheels of my wheelchair were in the air, and I fell with my head hitting the pavement. The bus was stopped, and the passengers offloaded. A fellow passenger had already called for an ambulance. While I waited lying on the pavement, it was freezing. Two policemen came over to me, took their jackets off and put them on me.

In Pakistan, there is better awareness now regarding disability, and we see the impact it is having in the society, but it is a very slight shift. In the past, there was no concept like this, and it was considered best for people like me to be kept at home. Gradually, society is being informed that people with disabilities have needs and desires and have a right to lead a normal life just like everyone else.

People in Pakistan who are disabled still face enormous difficulties. You hardly find any wheelchair access in public or private buildings. I often go to work in government offices without elevators or ramps, so my wheelchair has to be carried up 2-3 flights of stairs. My mobility and independence have only improved because I have bought a minivan, hired a driver as well as designed, and installed a ramp.

From my end, whenever I can, I highlight the issues of disability on many platforms, including social media. Whenever I can, I recommend that restaurants and all buildings should have barrier-free access when planned and provisions made for wheelchair access and for disabled toilets. In fact, I go to restaurants and ask that I should be provided wheelchair access as that is my right. Despite these challenges, I continue to be actively involved in raising awareness. I am involved with The National Forum for Women with Disabilities. It is a National Network of Disabled People's Organisations, with like-minded governmental and non-governmental local and international organisations, who all have women's disabilities as their mandate.

I was instrumental in circulating the bill on disability rights in the Azad Jammu and Kashmir Parliaments. It has been a year since its submission, and we are awaiting its result. Nowadays, disability rights issues, their awareness and legislation get a lot of attention in the media in Pakistan. This activism has led the government to register disability in the last national census and thus, grant the disabled the right to vote. With immense pride, I've cast my vote in the recent elections in Muzaffarabad. However, with great difficulty, as there is zero disability access in the building.

I was humbled to receive the Khadija Tul Kubra award in Islamabad by the speaker of the National Assembly of Pakistan. Khadija Tul Kubra was the wife of Prophet Muhammad (peace be upon him), who was also a successful businesswoman. It's an award based on extolling her virtues of courage, righteousness, and perfection in all relationships, making her a role model for all women. The Award recognises and honours the achievements and contributions of women with disabilities in Pakistan.

Recently, my interest has developed in the war on terrorism, and I would like to do my doctorate in this area of research. We all know that many lives have been affected in this war on terror. The majority of research studies so far mention and highlight veterans' mental health. Still, no sign has been given to the civilians who have been dumped into this whole mess and have suffered tremendously. I would like to investigate how those accused of being involved in terrorism are detained and tortured. After years of torture, many of them are proven not guilty and released back into society. Currently, my interest has also developed about the harmful effects of substance abuse. I plan to pursue this field and gain more education on its treatment and prevention.

Hina's story

I wonder how teachers could be so insensitive to my needs; wasn't it their job to cater to every student's needs? Were my needs so difficult or impossible? It was their attitude of not accepting me, which bothered me so much.

I was born and brought up in the metropolitan city of Karachi, Pakistan. Karachi is the capital of the Pakistani province of Sindh and is located on the coast of the Arabian sea. It is the largest city in Pakistan and the seventh largest in the world. It has a population of around 16 million people.

I am an only child, and my parents are doctors. My Abbu (father) is an Ear Nose and Throat surgeon (ENT), and my Ammi (mother) is a gynaecologist. I belong to a middle-class family, and I am my parents first born.

When I was nine months old, I was out with my father on a swing. For some reason, with him behind me, he called out my name, but got no response. He called me, again and again, but no response. He came before me, called me again, and I started laughing. He checked by clapping his hands, and with different sounds still got no response. He was confused and found the whole thing disturbing. Things looked strange as my father was sure something was wrong. He decided to do a hearing test on me, to confirm whether I had a hearing loss.

All this happened in the 1980s, when in Pakistan, healthcare facilities, including audiological testing, were not as up to date as they are today, and the latest hearing tests were not available. All my parents and the clinical practitioners who were looking after me knew that I had some hearing loss, but it was insufficient enough to require a treatment plan.

On the other hand, India had better audiological testing than Pakistan. Because my parents were in the medical field, they knew this, and when I was two years old, they took me to India. In India, I underwent an audiological assessment at the Shri Gagalbhai Audiology Clinic in Bombay, now known as Mumbai. An audiological evaluation is a series of diagnostic procedures used to determine the type, degree, and configuration of hearing loss. This evaluation aims to develop a unique treatment plan for each patient's need to improve their communication skills. After the initial assessment, the doctors found that I had 80% hearing loss in my right ear and 85% in my left.

Besides the initial assessment, the doctors gave my parents a plan of action covering areas of my education and lifestyle. My parents were not just guided step by step, but were counselled as well, which helped them to accept and understand my special need making them better placed to make informed decisions. Luckily, my parents being in the medical profession did not dwell and deny my condition, which is usually the denial phase in conditions like these, but agreed to the guidance and counsel the doctors gave. In addition, I was given a hearing aid which was accompanied by auditory training, without which I would not be able to use the aid. My parents were also guided on how the hearing aid should be used.

The clinic also strongly recommended that I be taught only one language, focusing on learning speech and no sign language, to enable me to speak fluently. They also suggested that I should be placed in a mainstream school and not a special school, as mainstream education would help me have a more normal education and assist me in gaining more speech. In those days, it was very difficult to get a hearing-impaired child into a mainstream school and this placed my parents in a very difficult position.

The first thing my parents did was to accept my disability; secondly, they faced the dilemma of whether to put me in a special school and lastly, the most challenging, getting me into a mainstream school, which after a great deal of effort, they were able to do.

Abbu and Ammi were not just medical professionals; they were pragmatic people. They got into action once they had accepted that I was born deaf. I guess they understood the gravity of the situation and how time was of the essence. Based on the recommendations, they devised a plan. The first step they took in implementing the goal was to start my speech therapy with a professional speech therapist. With everyone's hard work, I started speaking within a few months. Whilst my speech was fluent, it had a different sound, which I guess hearing people found a bit out of the ordinary.

The early intervention did play an important role, and by the age of three, I was in a mainstream pre- primary school. My speech therapy continued, my speech kept improving, and I talked fine in school. In those early years, individual attention and teaching on a one-to-one basis in small groups never created any problems for me. The following year I was in kindergarten, and there wasn't any problem. My teachers were friendly and understanding and never made me feel different. I cherish these memories, which were full of love and affection.

The problem arose when I got into class three. I was sent to the school's primary section, which completely changed my environment. The transition is difficult for any child my age as you move from a cocooned setting to a more open, colder, and indifferent one. So, with the changing of the premises, the whole scenario had changed for me. It was not that there were more students; there were few students, but the atmosphere was completely different. The other students in the class never bothered me, but the teachers had a problem with me being differently abled and this never set in well with them. They were uncooperative! In fact, they seemed to be after me. I don't know why? For example, when we used to do dictation in English or Urdu, they'd speak from behind me. I could lip-read well, but how could I from behind? They never listened to my request to face me while talking. As a result, I would get low marks in dictation. Also, whenever the teacher explained during a lesson, her face would be toward the blackboard, so whenever we used to have a question-answer session in class, I could never answer, because I couldn't understand what was being said. The teacher would say to me, 'you're such a duffer', but Alhamdulillah (praise be to Allah) I was not a duffer. These were very minor modifications I requested, but sadly none of the teachers ever complied.

I remember, once, a teacher made fun of my hearing aids and called them ugly! I was inconsolable after, and when I went home, I told Ammi. I kept asking her, *"why does no one else wear a hearing aid? Why do I have to wear it?"*. She could not answer me...She was speechless. The whole day, I did not eat anything and kept crying. She must have shared this incident with my father, so in the evening when he came home from work, he made me sit on his lap and asked why I was crying. I replied, *"I am crying because I wear a hearing aid, and nobody else wears one, everybody makes fun of me, and I don't want to wear it"*. My father reasoned with me and explained that all of us wear some kind of aid to help us. *"I wear glasses to help me see better, the same way you wear hearing aids to help you hear better, so does it make you or me a lesser human being?"*. Obviously, my answer was no; he further said, *"your father is an Ears Nose and Throat Surgeon, is anyone else's father that?"*. I said no. He said, then, *"you wear your hearing aid, and one day In Shaa Allah, you will be a surgeon like me!"*. After that day, I never cried and always wore my hearing aids; his words of wisdom consoled me and made me see another perspective.

I wonder how teachers could be so insensitive to my needs; wasn't it their job to cater to every student's needs? Were my needs so difficult or impossible? It was their attitude of not accepting me, which bothered me so much. The atmosphere in school and in society was very toxic, and even my neighbours were very hurtful. My parents and I had to bear a lot and I often had to put up with, *"you can't hear? Why do you talk like that?"*.

As a child, I had a fair complexion with curly hair and looked cute. A male teacher used to come to our home to teach the Holy Quran to some of my cousins, my neighbours' children and me. He used to touch me a lot. Obviously, there used to be other kids, but he would give them time off, and then touched me. This happened when I was four years old. He used to threaten me that, if I shared this with anyone, he would cut my hands. I was always so scared, and I remember once I nearly peed in my pants. When he went away, I took the courage and told my mother. She was shocked, and after that, I never saw him again. Because of this incident I became withdrawn, stopped going out to play, became anti-social, and was not willing to trust or touch anyone. In hindsight, telling children about good and bad touches is very important. I never knew about them and had to learn it the hard way. In these present times, these incidents are considered, sexual abuse.

Whenever I was disturbed, my speech would suffer and after this incident, I was quite shaken. Beside wetting the bed and becoming anti-social, I had significant issues and could not speak clearly or correctly. Since I was an only child, so much was expected of me. My parents, especially Ammi, wanted me to have perfect speech and this would add to my frustration. *"Speak correctly, speak clearly...."*, she would become very aggressive.

At that time, we were living in a joint family home and in this system, a family lives with all its members up to the second generation, including grandparents, parents, uncles, aunts, and their children. Children in this system, usually did not only play and study together, but were commonly compared to each other. Of course, this meant that children like me must work very hard to reach the level of my non- disabled cousins.

In Pakistani society, the woman is still blamed if the children are born disabled. Thankfully, my parents being doctors, avoided this false assumption, and I can now understand the tremendous pressure they were under with me as a disabled child.

These experiences were harsh for me, and they scarred me personally. Fortunately, Allah was kind to me, and I could gather myself and divert my energies towards my education as I wanted to do well and make my parents proud. I was a diligent worker, but my teachers were not allowing me to do well. My school was supposed to be a good school, but the teachers really bothered me a lot, they hurt me, and that used to cause problems.

My parents understood my plight, knew I was intelligent, and trusted my ability to work hard and do well. They made frequent visits to the school to try and make the principal and teachers understand, but it had no effect. In retrospect, I think my teachers didn't want to understand, because understanding would compel them to change. To say the least, their attitudes were so bad that if it wasn't for the understanding and support of my parents, I would not have withstood these challenges. Considering the circumstances, to make it easy for me, Ammi arranged a tuition teacher, so I found it easy to do homework with her. Believe me, if a normal/ hearing child had to do anything once, I had to do it ten times and work double hard.

It was very tough at school and emotionally very upsetting too. Once a teacher slapped me hard, leaving marks on my face. My hearing aid fell, I went home, and when Ammi saw my face and heard what happened, she was very distressed and went to my school and complained. Unfortunately, the complaining had an adverse effect as the teacher, instead of understanding, from that day on openly became my enemy. She would make sure that I got low marks in the subjects she taught. Despite all these setbacks, I continued to work hard and ploughed on. Alhamdulillah, when I finished, with Allah's blessing and my parent's support, I got a scholarship in matriculation.

In Pakistan, matriculation (usually referred to as "matric") is the term that refers to the final examinations that take place at the end of the 9th and 10th grades. It results in awarding a Secondary School Certificate (SSC). The examinations are conducted by the secondary school board and not by an individual school. I was among the top 10 students and was awarded a cash prize. It meant that my road to success was hard, treacherous, and yet achievable. It also proved that hard work gets recognised, and even though my school and teachers did not accept my hard work and disability, others did!

One phase of my educational era had now passed, and I entered a new phase when I gained admission to a college in premedical/science. The transition from school to college life opened new challenges for me. Since it was a large institution with thousands of students, nobody was personally concerned about anyone. In some ways, it was good as nobody picked up on my disability as they did in school, but nevertheless, things were tough. There was an influx of students, and the classrooms were not large enough to accommodate all of us. For some subjects, many of us had to sit on the floor and were not physically present in the classroom. Imagine me with my hearing problem, with no view to lipread the person talking. Most of the times, in the classes I sat in, I couldn't understand what was happening, what the students were saying, as they were all not facing me.

Just like my primary and secondary years of education, it was necessary for me to have home tuition to understand what was happening in class. I stayed with the same tuition teacher from class three until I became a dentist. She was a gem; she was like my second mother, always there for me and supporting me. She was my anchor, friend, and confidante and was a very important part of my life. She taught me never to surrender during all those trials and tribulations I faced. Sometimes, not in front of my parents, but in front of her, I would give up a little...you know, all of this was so emotionally draining that I thought I could never do it. She never let me feel that I could not succeed. Constantly she motivated me and pushed the bars higher every time so that I could reach the skies.

Since both Abbu and Ammi were in medicine, I also wanted to become a doctor, which is why I had chosen premedical subjects in my intermediate studies. After the results came out, the question arose as to which field of medicine I would like to pursue. My parents wanted to know my preference, but I in turn looked up to my father for guidance. He suggested that since there is no dental surgeon in the family, perhaps I should pursue dentistry, and I agreed. He accompanied me when I went for my interview at the dental college. We had a candid exchange with the principal about my needs and limitations and I promised that I would work hard and give my one hundred per cent. The principal agreed, and I was granted admission. I was never given any special concessions or privileges during my studies and was always made to do the same as the hearing students.

Looking back, I think we should have requested minor modifications to make my journey easier.

Society's attitudes were strange and challenging on my small step to gain admission to a dental college. One would think throughout the years that people might be happy after seeing my struggle. On the contrary, many people had different opinions about me. *"Oh my God, how will she become a dentist? How will she cope? Better to let her do a simple BA degree".* All these negative comments and suggestions put a lot of pressure on my parents and me.

Ironically, nobody around me at the dental college, including the professors, teachers and students, was ready to believe that I had a problem; they thought I was playing up. Yes, according to their observation, I looked normal, acted normal, and spoke quite normal, but they forgot that I could not hear well. My speech therapy as an early intervention proved to be very beneficial; I could speak and read lips very well. The pitfall was that people were unwilling to believe that I could still not hear well, and for me to be able to read their lips, I had to see them speaking, and not just hear them from behind, as hearing people can!! Unfortunately, I faced the same dilemma: educators at all levels could not understand my needs and make those minimal provisions that would have helped me. My fellow students understood my predicament, although a few, I know, found me annoying. They didn't like how I talked. They had difficulty understanding my speech, and I know, as young people they didn't have the kind of patience and insight to understand other people's problems.

The lights would be switched off during the lectures, so I couldn't understand anything. I could only lipread when I was facing the person talking. I requested either not to switch off the lights or to let me sit in the front row, so I could see and lipread the teacher delivering the lecture. Unfortunately, none of these requests were ever granted. Then again, during classes, the lecturer would ask me a question. I would not understand the question as questions and answers were in the darkness, and I wouldn't understand them. All the lecturers had to do was talk to me, nothing special; just look at me and speak by coming close to me.

It was so frustrating...I didn't know what to do...nobody paid heed to my repeated requests to solve my problem. I used to take help from my father, but he was busy sometimes and couldn't give me time. My tuition teacher was my saviour; she would always assist, even with simple stuff, like the meaning of words. Also, she would search them, read them and help me. Despite struggling in many ways, I still tried to help my classmates a lot, but I never got help in return. I had a very small circle of friends who accepted and understood my special need and they were very sincere.

In the first year of my medical studies, I remember in my oral examination I was questioned on a one-to-one basis. I answered all the questions. The professor was surprised he said, *"you didn't know anything whenever you were asked during the lectures, and how come you know everything now?"*. I said, *"sir, before you used to ask me in a dark lecture hall and I couldn't understand, now you are asking me in a lighted room and facing me"*. He just brushed this off as nonsense; he or the other teachers were unwilling to realise their mistakes and shortcomings on how their actions or inaction adversely affected me. Some of my teachers did not like me, because I repeatedly asked questions until it was clear. I noticed that, usually, they explained it to the other students but not me. I remember one female teacher; I couldn't understand what she was saying as she would talk very fast and in a low tone. If I used to ask her to write the points from her lecture down for me, she would get angry at me. During my four years in medical college, I got the minimum marks in her subject. The same approach continued throughout the years of medical studies. Still, I guess I grew resilient and adapted myself to the prevailing conditions, and rather than complaining, I just got on with working hard and trying to reach the targets that I had set for myself. Some teachers used to be good, and some were outright rude.

After the final year examinations, it was the time of my viva, (oral examination) which was again a problem. During the viva, when questions were asked, if I did not understand, I would request them to repeat the question, but they would say you do not know and ask the next question immediately. I would plead with them, *"please understand I cannot hear like you', but no one was listening!"*. None of this would even be considered an extraordinary request, it was just simple consideration. The result was that my marks were low, which was very depressing! I used to look at my parents and know that I had to be strong for them, as they had faced so much for me. They would go weak when they saw me depressed, especially Ammi. She had developed tremors in her hands and feet, and I wanted to make her and my father proud, as their struggles were mine and they had always been there for me.

The four years at dental college were full of pitfalls and challenges, but they did pass; I sailed through, and came out as a dental surgeon! The fifth year is the house job, the critical year under supervision before starting as a dental physician. This next chapter brought new hurdles as I faced sexual harassment.

I distinctly remember there was a professor in the department, he made my life hell. Wearing a mask, he would ask me a question in front of the patients. Because I could not hear or read his lips, obviously I could not answer. He would insist that I did not know the answer. Also, whenever I asked him anything, he would never explain or answer, and would say, *"go do it yourself, do not ask me; you never understand what I'm saying"*.

You can't imagine how he ridiculed me, but I never told my parents about it as I did not want to upset them. I had to spend three months in that department, and he made sure those were very tough for me. I felt I was losing it and would go into depression, but I kept going. On top of this belittling behaviour, he used to make sure that I did not get any cases, publicly announcing that I did not know anything. So, I never used to get a patient.

I tried to make him understand, but he was unwilling to change. This could be considered a classic example of workplace harassment, but I could not even complain, because no one was willing to understand.

Another professor from another department I thought understood my problem, but he tried to take advantage of the situation. He would shower cheap praises and compliment me on my looks, accompanied by threats that he would fail me, if I did not listen to him. Being good-looking did not help, as people around me were always there to take advantage of my situation. You can term it sexual harassment in the workplace. What bothered me the most was the idea in people's minds that just because I was deaf, I have no brains or conscience and would be willing to compromise my values. To say the least, I do not have good memories of my teachers. In fact, they still haunt me!!

I became very aggressive at this time, and my relationship with people close to me suffered terribly. I had no one to talk to who would understand and who I could explain my frustrations to. Rejection made me feel frustrated and I became very angry and developed severe anger issues. Nobody around me could understand, not even my parents as to why I was having these problems and why I was behaving the way I did. When I think back, I realise that I probably needed counselling to help me keep on track.

Since I am an only child, there were no siblings to share my emotions with. I had a friend who I was able to share some stuff, but I guess that was not enough; I needed more, I was looking for a friend, a partner who I could share my life with, but I found out that people in the two instances I encountered, were not serious when it came to the next level of commitment after befriending someone. In our culture and religion, the next level of commitment is marriage. I never believed in just having a relationship for the heck of it. Of course, such episodes added to the rejections I felt, and they negatively impacted on me, affecting my self-esteem, which was already bruised.

I was born a Muslim, I'm very religious and I always find peace and solace in my namaz - the obligatory five times prayer a day Muslims make. When I was at the lowest peak, I suddenly stopped praying. I felt spiritually disconnected, I was lonely, was angry, had no friends, was heartbroken and felt rejected. My teachers, colleagues, and supposed friends, all played a part in this. They are all mortals, and it may not have mattered much to them, but I felt that even Allah wasn't listening to me, and I thought, why should I continue praying?

I tried to involve myself in some hobbies, like cooking and reading to come out from this pool of negativity which was engulfing me. I found joy in trying out new recipes for my parents and family and just loved the thought that it pleased the people who ate them. As for books, they have been my best friends since my childhood. Whenever I was upset, or something disturbed me, I would take refuge in a book and get instant comfort. I was always fond of reading novels both in English and Urdu as I was fluent in both. Then, a friend told me to read the book *Peer e Kamil*. I did not want to read it, but my friend urged me to. I started reading that novel, and I never looked back. It is about a woman's spiritual journey and how she gains eternal satisfaction and success. While reading it, I could resonate with the character; this completely changed my outlook and was genuinely beneficial in recreating my connection with my creator.

All the disconnected cords were reconnected, and my bond was strong this time. I understood many things that in the past I could not; I was able to delve deeper into my soul and could understand why Allah chose me for this life. I started paying more attention to what Allah wanted from me rather than what I wanted from him. After that, I held onto Allah, and I started praying namaz and *tahujjud* - **prayers during the night**.

I had rekindled the bond with my creator and when I began praying, it helped me stabilise myself; all those negative thoughts of anger, frustration, and rejection slowly and gradually started to phase out. I started feeling not just better but, in a way, reformed and rejuvenated. I also started accepting the reality as I had always done in the past. I believe worry is a conversation about things you cannot change. Prayer is a conversation you have with Allah about something he can change.

I was 23 years old when I started my house job, and I was 25 years old when I started working. The entry into professional life was again riddled with senseless and baseless assumptions. Everyone was like, *"how will you communicate with your patients?"*. My answer was just like how I communicate with you and everyone. They would say, *"that is ok, we do understand you, but will your patients be able to understand?"*. My answer to them was, *"it is my problem; I will manage it"*.

I did not have a problem communicating with my patients when I started working at the dental clinic in my father's medical centre. Patients have had no issues communicating with me or how I undertook their treatment. They appreciated my commitment and skills; according to most of them, whenever they saw me, half of their worries went away just by looking at me and talking with me. This appreciation boosted my confidence and motivated me to continue. With this confidence, I could deal with stray derogatory comments like, *"you poor thing"*, and I would think, why are they calling me a poor thing? I'm treating them, I'm their doctor! What is there to pity me? By the Grace of Allah Almighty, I continued to surpass all the hurdles, gaining my patient's appreciation and praise, and proving my opponents wrong.

Since I was an only child, people assumed things were tailor-made for me...and I kept receiving the cake...no!! The journey has been treacherous, and I have been through hell. Whilst I had to carve out opportunities for myself, when I was given a chance, I gave it two hundred per cent. I should say all that I've been able to achieve so far, is a combination of hard work and determination on my part, plus the guidance and patience of my parents.

In Pakistan today, there is much better awareness of people with disabilities than before, but there is still a long way to go. To start with, I would like to see the non-disabled show a little humility to people with disabilities, not be judgmental, rather than pitying they should be able to empathise with them. I would like them to be in our shoes; I would like them to feel how we feel, to not be able to communicate with others. It will not take a lot, just a little patience, a little motivation, a little understanding, a little compassion, and little opportunities. That is all we are asking!! Disability should be taken as a different form of ability. With certain modifications, it's a matter of giving equal opportunities to the disabled in education, health, employment and in daily living. Pakistan needs to enter the 21st century with the disabled accepted as part of the nation's workforce.

I was in my late twenties in full-time employment, financially independent and had entered the phase in life where a girl in eastern Muslim society is supposed to get married. In Pakistani society twenties are the peak years for a girl to get married. I was still single, which according to the societal norms, was worrisome. The girls and their parents are usually under tremendous pressure to tie the knot. In a traditional arranged marriage, the boy's side usually comes to propose to the girl. Afterwards, the girl's side consents or says no to the proposal. Parental involvement from both sides is the key in such situations.

In my situation, proposals used to come as I was blessed with good education, family and Allah had blessed me with good looks as well, and most importantly, I was also the only child. Unfortunately, this was not enough, as whenever a proposal would come, the main issue would be my disability, a matter of grave concern for the boy and the family. Nobody would look at my accomplishments and see me as a whole person. According to general standards, it was not acceptable to have a wife/daughter-law who is deaf!!

Besides me being differently abled, families making a proposal to my family, kept asking about *Jahez*. The tradition of *Jahez* has its roots in the culture of the Indian subcontinent. It has no connection to the religion of Islam.

Jahez can comprise durable goods, cash, jewellery and real or movable property, vehicles and other household items that help the newlyweds set up their home that the bride's family gives to the groom, his parents and his relatives as a condition of the marriage.

These practices still continue in countries like Pakistan, India and Bangladesh. Despite many countries having banned these customs and punishment is granted for such acts, corruption prevails. Hence many people do not take this seriously. Sometimes it can be a direct demand. In the so-called civilised society, there is an indirect reference to specific demands put forward by the groom's family, which are supposed to be fulfilled by the bride's family. This places an undue burden on the girl's family. Many parents to get their daughters married go down the road of obtaining loans from people, getting interest-based loans from banks, using their life savings, and even selling their homes.

I underwent this type of demands and conditions, and those who came to me with a proposal, were always interested in what my parents had to offer in terms of *Jahez*. They would not be ashamed to ask whose name the house is in. *"You have only one daughter? what will you give her when she gets married?"*. These questions were asked usually in a very non-embarrassing way. It seemed they were entering into a business deal rather than holy matrimony!

My father had taken this very bold step and set up a condition that greedy people should not be invited to come home and make demands, but at the same time, the pressure was mounting on my parents to get me married. People used to advise my parents to just do it regardless of the boy or the family, just for the heck of getting married. With all my cousins married, my mother was so depressed, *"what will happen, what to do? When we die, what will happen to you?"*. These kinds of thoughts worried her constantly.

Yes, I was well educated and financially independent, but another couple of years had passed, and I was still single; it was a time of great despair. Then I got a proposal from a distant relative on my mother's side, but it was not thought to be compatible as he was not well educated, so he was refused.

Another year passed, and I was now 30 years old; the guy whose proposal was rejected approached me on social media. At that time, he was pursuing his master's degree in philosophy. He was also working full-time with a moderate income. We started talking, and he said he was interested in me after a while. I offered to meet him in person, so he could see me with all my particular needs, as I was hurt in the past and did not want to be hurt again. He declined my offer, which made me think optimistically about him. He was the only one who did not judge me at all; he did not ask me simple questions, nor did he want me to satisfy his mother or other family members. The more we talked, the more barriers were crossed, and we shared our challenges and achievements.

After both of us had consented, he and his family came up with the proposal for the second time. His parents were not highly educated, nor were they from a very well-off background, but they came in a dignified manner. No stupid questions were asked, no one was embarrassed or put on the spot, and the proposal was accepted solemnly. On his request, instead of an engagement, our *Nikah* was done. In Islamic law, marriage – or, more specifically, the marriage contract – is called *Nikah*. This Arabic word is already in the Quran and is used exclusively to refer to the arrangement of marriage. Our *rukhsati*, which is the acceptance of Nikah, took place after a year.

Marriage has had a positive effect, and both of us are proving good for each other. My husband wasn't well settled at the time of marriage, but with time, he became well settled. I am not materialistic and accepted the way he is, and in return, he also accepted me wholeheartedly. I was looking for love with sincerity and companionship, which I've received in abundance. When we started our lives together, he began to understand my problem; he was shocked to know how much I've gone through! We now share everything with each other and have developed that level of understanding where we give comfort and motivate each other to achieve and appreciate what we have together. After marriage, he did his second master's in audiology/special education/speech pathology and is now employed in the audiology department at a good hospital.

We do face challenges now as well, but we manage them together. He works full time, and I have opted for part-time work, because of my home responsibilities. Alhamdulillah I'm very happy and Allah has blessed me with two beautiful daughters. He has given me a reward for the hardships that I have gone through since childhood, I see them as a blessing. I want the best for my daughters, and I don't want them to go through what I have gone through.

Nuzhat's story

There I was mentally very sharp; my sisters were going to school, and I wasn't allowed to. Can you imagine the havoc this played with my mind? It was a miserable and depressing feeling...

I was born in the urban city of Lahore, Pakistan. Lahore is the capital of the Pakistani province of Punjab, the country's second largest city after Karachi, and the twenty sixth largest in the world. My father was a major in the Pakistan Army, so he had postings every two years, which meant that we moved home frequently. In a way that enriched our childhood experiences, with new places and adventures. We are four sisters, and I am the third, with a younger sister and two older ones.

As far as my mother remembers, my birth was normal. She used to say that I was diagnosed with polio when I was one and a half years. Poliomyelitis, commonly shortened to polio, is an infectious disease that is caused by the poliovirus. In about 0.5 per cent of cases, it moves from the gut to affect the central nervous system and muscle weakness results in flaccid paralysis. This can occur over a few hours to a few days. The defect most often involves the legs, but may less commonly involve the head, neck and diaphragm muscles. Many people fully recover. In those with muscle weakness, about 2 to 5 per cent of children and 15 to 30 per cent of adults die. For all those infected, there are no symptoms in up to 70 per cent of infections. Another 25 per cent, have minor symptoms, such as fever and a sore throat, whilst up to 5 per cent have a headache, stiffening of the neck, and pains in the arms and legs. These people are usually back to normal within one or two weeks. However, years after recovery, the post-polio syndrome may occur, with muscles becoming weak, similar to that of a person with an initial infection. Obviously, I do not remember anything being so young.

I can imagine it must have been a great setback for my parents when I was diagnosed with polio. After the diagnosis, my lower limbs rapidly got affected, meaning I had no sensation from my waist down to my feet, and I was unable to walk. My mother would carry me and take me every day for massages and whatever treatments that were available. I am told I underwent many treatments, but unfortunately, my situation/ disability could not be reversed. You can imagine sixty years ago what must have been the situation when polio was so rampant, and there were no vaccines available.

The vaccine immunization programme in Pakistan started in the 1970s, but only began to be appropriately implemented in the 1990s. Polio has been eradicated in all continents except Asia, and as of 2022, unfortunately, Afghanistan and Pakistan are the only two countries where the disease is still classified as endemic. Despite the disease being preventable with the polio vaccine, in my case, none of the treatments or therapies has worked. I was nearly four years old when it was accepted that I had polio and would never be able to walk again.

When it was time for me to start kindergarten, I couldn't be admitted to the school because of my disability. There were a couple of reasons: we did not have a wheelchair or resources, like having a carer to push my wheelchair, nor did schools have the kind of provision needed like ramps and barrier-free access. I was so disturbed, and there was so much longing in me to go to school.

There I was mentally very sharp; my sisters were going to school, and I wasn't allowed to. Can you imagine the havoc this played with my mind? Around me, all my sisters were going to school, and I was left behind. It was a miserable and depressing feeling.

As a manifestation of this, I used to be very short-tempered and would easily get irritated and agitated. The brunt of my frustration I would take out on my younger sister, who is five years my junior. If she didn't listen to me, I would be very aggressive towards her and scratch her or throw whatever I could get hold of at her. I would beat her up. This is how I vented my emotions. My parents felt helpless in this whole scenario. No matter how much they pleaded and begged, the schools were unwilling to understand, and we were left with no choice.

My parents were conscious of this lacking and the adverse effects it could have on me emotionally and psychologically, so my father, as compensation, started to tutor me at home. Since childhood, I have had a very sharp mind with good grasping power. My father would give me a lot of attention and concentrate on me. He would get me books, and with his hard work and my perseverance combined, I did get up to the mark of the normal grade levels as my other sisters. My mother also helped, but the major chunk of homeschooling was done by my father. He was very focused on my studies, and I did reciprocate by giving my 100%. At the same time, because of the homeschooling and positive atmosphere, I developed into a very confident child.

Meanwhile, my sisters were equally supportive, no outing was done without me, and whenever I did need to be carried, it would be done without any complaints. The most comforting part was how well my parents and sisters had accepted my special need and understood how to deal with it. My eldest sister, who was five years older than me, would carry me in her lap as her duty.

Even though we had an average living and a lot of economic strains, our upbringing was solid, and our parents tried to instill positive traits and values in us. They brought us up in a way where my sisters were very caring, and we greatly loved each other. I was never regarded as lesser, or my disability was never an issue within our small loving family. Most importantly, my parents never had any gender bias toward their daughters. They never thought as we are girls, we should be placed in a corner. They were equally supportive of all their daughters, and I was never made to feel different from my sisters. This is the reason for my confidence. In fact, they are the ones who took great pride in every minor achievement of mine and never felt embarrassed to display their appreciation in front of others. This positive environment had a trickledown effect on my extended family and relatives as they had to accept me. As a family, we were so close-knit and strong that nobody dared to display any negativity towards me or my disability.

During the early years, we had certain financial constraints, and my parents could not afford a wheelchair for me. I used to have a tricycle, and having some movement in my legs, I used to push it, but I couldn't drive it. When I was nearly ten, my Nani (maternal grandmother) and some other close relatives sold their gold and bought me a wheelchair. You can imagine my joy in acquiring my mobility, and with that came my freedom to openly move around. At that time, my father was posted as a station commander in Lahore. Years had passed, and I was ten years old. Around this time, I had been taught at home so well that I could have managed studies at grade five level. Grade five is middle school, so my parents again started approaching schools for my admission. Lahore being a mega city, I thought it would have opportunities for me.

On the contrary, such is the mindset of our society at large and the very restrictive schooling systems that there was still an unwillingness on the part of schools to grant me admission. The easiest and the lamest excuse school principals made was that I should continue with homeschooling, for if I were admitted in a school, I might be bothered by the other children. At this stage, I was very confident in myself, and after a lot of convincing and cajoling, I was admitted to a mainstream school in grade four.

So, at the age of 10, my dream of going to a school like my sisters and friends finally came true, and I was able to step into a real school. I cannot explain the feelings I had at this moment. It was a pure and simple joy; I had waited so many years for this moment. You know how a sportsman trains, and then one day he is left in the arena to face the opponent and the crowd. I was a bit shy and scared at this new stage in my life, but my self-confidence soon took over. The school's environment was conducive to learning, and with another girl with special needs, I was well accepted, which further helped boost my self-confidence. My father was a station commander at this time, and the area schools came under him. Owing to his forward thinking, he built ramps from his own money around the school so I could access the building independently, unless there were stairs to be climbed. In class, I sat in the front row.

Of course, there were always problems, big and small, but there were solutions too. During my school years, I made some very good friends who were very helpful and loyal, so that time passed well, leaving me with some beautiful memories. I was very social both in and outside school and had a lot of friends. Years passed, and I did my matriculation (10th grade). A matriculation certificate is issued to one who has cleared 9th and 10th grade. I was a bright, hardworking, student, very independent, did well in my studies and my examination results were also good.

My school years were good; it was a memorable journey. Like my sisters and friends, I was looking forward in anticipation after my matriculation to start college for my intermediate 11th and 12th grade. In my mind, the stage was set for me to get admission to a good college as my school results were good. But lo and behold, I could not access any good college. The main reason was accessibility, and the good colleges where I wanted to study were far from where we lived, and there was no public transport providing for a wheelchair. Secondly, we could not afford a car and driver to take me to college, neither could we afford the transport cost, if we hired a private taxi. My passion was to do a degree in home economics and become financially independent, but these issues dampened my dreams and desires. Every new phase in my life bought a new barrage of barriers and challenges to face.

At this point, I had to settle for a college that was near our residence, but it was an Urdu speaking one, whilst I had been educated in an English medium school.

The academic situation in Pakistan regarding the language of instruction is very divided. Pakistan was formerly a part of the Indian subcontinent, which has been over the centuries ruled by different invaders. Before its disintegration, in the mid-1900s, its last rulers were the British. The colonial British had introduced English as a medium of instruction in all the private schools of the subcontinent. Constitutionally, Urdu has been declared the national language of Pakistan since its independence in 1947. However, regrettably, this remains mostly on paper, and realistically the country still struggles in many areas to unchain itself from the clutches of its colonial past.

We are now in the 75th year of independence, but there is still widespread recognition that English is the language of power. Among the children of well-to-do parents the 'Urdu medium' is almost an insult. Kids understand early on that Urdu is the language you use to order servants, while English is used by their parents to communicate with friends and family. Poorer parents also get this message and sacrifice their meagre resources to pay for their children to study in so-called 'English-medium' schools. Intelligence counts for little as it is assumed that, if you can speak English fluently, you must be bright and from a well-connected family. So, you start life with a distinct advantage, looking down on those less fortunate people whose accent identifies them as *Urdu medium*.

Since I had attended a private school, I was used to English as a medium of instruction. Also, for the reasons mentioned above, I felt as if I was demoted when against all this backdrop, I had to settle for an Urdu medium college. However, the reasons were accessibility and lack of financial resources. It was frustrating being caught in this linguistic arrogance that divides our society. All the lectures were delivered in Urdu, and I had to take notes in Urdu. None of my friends opted for this college, so I also lost my friends. Each day I would drag myself to college and attend classes. I would very irritably come home, translate the lectures from Urdu into English, and then prepare for the next class. As expected, I lost motivation to study further because of this. College, for me, was a mere form of attendance to get my Bachelor of Arts degree. I had aimed higher and wanted to achieve something more in life, enter a professional field and make a name for myself, but I was denied this opportunity.

I used to go to college with my wheelchair, an old style manual one. This I did every day with my friends. I was blessed with good friends who would accompany me daily on foot instead of taking public transport.

However, while I was in the first year of my studies, I was spotted by Abbas (my husband-to-be), an army cadet who was posted in Lahore. I don't know where he saw me, but we were introduced to each other through mutual friends. We were both nineteen, got talking, and a friendship developed, which became a turning point in my life.

After a while, Abbas was posted to another city. He was serious about our friendship and wanted a long-term commitment. He was an only son with two sisters, one older and one younger. His desire was for us to get engaged, but he had family responsibilities to fulfil and wanted to get his sisters married off first. In Pakistani culture, it is always the oldest son's responsibility with his father to get the daughters/sisters married off. He was very aware of his obligations to his family, but at the same time, he did not want to lose me and wanted a commitment. Obviously, his parents had reservations about my disability, and thought as we were both young and emotional, this kind of relationship would not last. His family was not willing that he should commit to someone so early in his life, but he was adamant, and after much persuasion, his parents agreed. It took him two years to make his parents understand that he was seriously committed and to make them agree to his choice.

The situation was that, whilst his parents had consented after some time at his insistence, my parents were totally against Abbas and I being together. My father talked to me extensively and repeatedly explained the downsides of this decision. He thought it would not last and wanted to save me from the trauma of being left by Abbas after the love wore off. People also tried explaining to Abbas that I might not be able to bear any children, which is an integral part of any marriage. Their view was that, if you are aware of these realities, then, why would you knowingly want to get into something that will end in disaster. My father also tried to explain all the pros and cons to Abbas. He was being realistic as he believed that we were young and emotional. He also shared with Abbas his biggest fear, saying, *"you are not thinking of my daughter, and when you leave her later, she will be more hurt, so it's better that you disappear now"*. Adamantly, Abbas stood his ground and after many arguments and disagreements, we finally got engaged. Both my parents were realistic and cautiously remained concerned for my welfare. They wanted to save their beloved daughter from any future heartbreak and trauma. I guess Abbas and I had faith in Allah Almighty and our strong perseverance won through.

In a typical Islamic and Pakistani culture, the boy's parents are given the honour of going to the girl's family with their son's proposal, which is what Abba's parents did. In this way, I was saved from going through the ritual of entertaining marriage proposals from the opposite sex. It usually happens in our Pakistani culture that proposals of eligible boys start coming when a girl becomes of marriageable age. It remains a very cumbersome ritual in our society. So, meeting and choosing Abbas as my life partner in the initial years saved me from going through this awkward journey.

We got engaged, and our engagement stood for nine years. When I say stood, this is, to say the least, as these were very turbulent years. These years stood the test of time, and although both of us faced many challenges, our love and understanding grew stronger with each passing year. Abbas even took my elder sister as his confidante and by the time we were married twelve years later, he had risen from a cadet to the rank of a major.

Our marriage was finally decided once Abbas had gotten the sisters married off. I had spent the last nine years anticipating this event. On the one hand, I felt excited about getting married, yet on the other hand, the feeling of unpredictability was also there. All I was confident of was Abbas's love for me as I knew how much I loved him. I remember at the time of our wedding, his uncle and even some of his army seniors suggested that he reconsider. They told him he could call off the marriage, if he decided to do so, but Abbas kept his promise and did not budge. Our society looks at marrying a disabled person as a form of charity. It's a good deed, a noble gesture, but quite unthinkable that this can lead to an everyday happy life. Because of this, some people believe that even though it's noble to marry a disabled, the husband should take a second wife to have a normal life.

There were many preconceived notions before we married; the most troubling one was my inability to conceive, compelling my mother-in-law to seek a medical opinion, which was given in the negative. It was understandable where she was coming from and had all the mother's apprehensions for her child. She was further subjected to baseless suggestions that since her daughter-in-law was disabled, if she ever did conceive, there was the chance that her offspring might have some form of disability, or her polio may be passed on to her child.

Another baseless assertion was people informing my mother-in-law of the opinion that she was getting her son married off in a family where they are all girls (we are four sisters), so I might also have girls only. These ideas do not have any medical basis as such. My husband Abbas is quite snobbish, so people never pass comments like these in front of him. He is quite rude and blunt; he would just snub if he heard something like this. As to his mother, he comforted and satisfied her, so people backed off gradually.

Married life was good, and Abbas and I were finally enjoying each other's company and planning on the journey we were going to make together. It had been a long wait for us, so we were revelling in our time together. As to the attitude of people around us, we were so happy within ourselves, and everything was so settled that we couldn't care; our positive stance towards life was the winning factor.

Settling down after our marriage came with many challenges. My parents' house was well adapted to my disability and had good wheelchair access. As Abbas had postings every couple of years, it was always army accommodation we were in, and these were not custom-built; hence they were not always disabled-friendly. Accessibility/barrier- free access was one of the major issues I experienced in these residences. At times we would get a house where my wheelchair would not go in the bathroom. He used to carry me in and carry me out after using the toilet and bathing, just like how you do with a child. In the beginning, we could not afford the physical changes due to our finances, then slowly, this improved which helped us to manage our accessibility requirements. Once I had overcome these physical hurdles, life was beautiful and relatively smoother. The constant factor in these situations was the support I got from Abbas, which kept me going.

By the will of Allah Almighty, all the sceptics were proven wrong, and I was pregnant in the first few months of our marriage. Abbas and I were very excited when we got the good news. Still, the cynics throughout my pregnancy never stopped creating doubts by passing negative comments like, *"anything can go wrong, you are sitting all the time, how do you get some exercise etc"*. On the contrary, I was not anxious at all! Truthfully, from day one, I had left it to Allah. I had faith that, if Allah is with me and if this was meant to happen, it would happen, and if it was not his will, then it was not going to happen.

As a divine sign, things started happening in my favour. My pregnancy was so good and easy that you cannot imagine. With such a big tummy, I would do everything till the last moment. In fact, Abbas was not even there, as he had been posted to Quetta, and I was in Lahore with my parents. Everything happened so fast that I had my first daughter before our first anniversary. My daughter Sarah was a prize - winning baby. Allah does help when you ask him.

After Sarah's birth, again came the apprehensions about bringing up my own child! These apprehensions always came from outsiders. My own family never had any doubts about me. I was always a very hard worker, even before my marriage. I was very creative; I was an excellent cook, a good tailor, and had good home management skills. I even had brought up my niece and nephew from the beginning, as my sister had a full-time job.

After Sarah, we were blessed with another daughter Zara. Bringing up my own children was never a problem. Abbas, at this time, was posted to Quetta, which meant that I was in Quetta all on my own. In those days, telephone communication was not as good as it is today and there were no mobile phones. We felt cut off from our family, but after three months we got a break to visit them in Lahore.

When we used to have postings every two years, half of the people were envious of us, and half were inquisitive about our home situation and wondered how we coped. Then slowly things would become normal, and people were not as inquisitive as we got to know each other.

We didn't face any obvious negativity when the time came for the girls to go to school, but there were instances when they would be asked questions like, *"how come your mother uses a wheelchair, how does she bathe you, feed you?"*. My children would answer honestly that I did all this work myself. The initial introduction to their friends or their families and their reactions around the first meeting put the girls on guard. I guess it was more intrigue than ridicule. Once the initial introductions were done, the girls did not care; they grew more confident and took pride in me as their mother.

As a mother, I was always involved in the girls' education; I tutored them. I was the one who attended all their PTAs etc. and took part in all their activities. Overall, my girls were dependent on me. At times they felt that their lives since childhood were stable, and this made them confident. They looked at this as a blessing and as well as their parents being in a long-lasting relationship.

Masha Allah, *(What God has willed)* they are bright and good girls. The eldest, Sarah, did her Master's, and the younger one, Zara, has done her BSc and her Master's in Australia. Zara and I are partners in our cake-making business. I have been quite creative and am always inclined to do different innovative things, so she probably inherited this creativity from me. It is a thriving business, and we work on orders and operate from home.

In our society, the in-laws have reservations about going to meet a girl for their son. In Sarah's case, Usman (her husband) was her classmate, and they had liked each other and so we were happy with her choice when her husband parents came with their proposal. They might have had reservations about Sarah having a disabled mother who used a wheelchair, but when they first met us and saw how I manage my household, they were full of praise. Moreover, they didn't find any shortcomings in Sarah, which would have hindered their decision. I have two beautiful granddaughters, and even to this day, when they come to my house, bathing, feeding them, is my responsibility.

I was lucky enough to get very good support from my family, who were educated and aware. They are the ones who instilled in me confidence and never felt embarrassed by my disability. In fact, they would make sure that my name would be mentioned in front of the guests visiting; they would always be proud of me, and even when it wasn't needed, they would take them around and show them my creativity and artwork. Likewise, my sisters' attitude was always sisterhood, never pity, more friendship and kinship, to say the least. For example, my sister Riffat is a good orator, so whenever I took part in a debate, she was the first one to write down points for me, make me learn my stuff and then push me to speak on stage. Similarly, I am much adored by all my in-laws. Everybody talks about me with fondness, and nobody feels that I'm disabled and unable to do anything.

My disability never came in the way of looking after everyone, maintaining relationships, kinship ties, etc.

Similarly, I have been lucky to have good friends; you can hardly find such kind these days. My college was nearly a mile and a half from my residence. I had no transport facilities, so I would go in my wheelchair, and my friends would walk and accompany me and push my wheelchair instead of using any transport. My cousins were also very supportive and caring. I also had a lot of endurance; I was not the sensitive type to cry about everything. If I could not do something, I would take it in my stride and be realistic and practical rather than moan and groan. For example, if we went to the beach, it was obviously impossible to take my wheelchair on the sand. So, if I were sitting on a beach, some of my cousins would sit with me for hours, and we would chat and enjoy ourselves. This, in my opinion, was a great sacrifice on their part. Even now, if I cannot go somewhere, they will also not go; for example, our cinemas do not have elevators or escalators. The cinema people have made provision for me to sit at the front of the screen and watch a movie. It is no joy to watch a movie this way, but my friends and family will insist and sit with me, even though I urge them to go and watch the film from a better position.

My being in a wheelchair has never deterred me or my family or friends from socialising or going on vacations. Sometimes there is a lack of facilities for wheelchair users, but my husband will carry me uphill, of course, supported by our friends.

Today in Pakistan, there is more awareness about disability, but we have yet to think about our disabled when government and business are drawing up and implementing their plans. We have severe accessibility issues in our country, where barrier-free access is not considered a priority. For example, I face huge problems when I go to see my eye specialist in a major hospital where the doorways are so narrow that, every time, they have to readjust some furniture to make space for my wheelchair. Now, this is a hospital I'm talking about; can you imagine other regular buildings?

Barrier-free access in construction and equal

opportunities for inclusion in education and the workforce are major areas that have been ignored and need proper focus. We are in the 21st century, but society still fails to see us as part of the mainstream; instead, the focus is on our wheelchairs/disabilities. We are usually perceived as pitiful objects; a curse from God. People with disability have been severely dumped, and some of the attitudes and challenges unfortunately, remain the same, as when I was a young child with polio sixty years ago!

Tanzila's story

A nasty comment. 'Disabled people use their disability as a get-away by playing the sympathy card to get a lot of opportunities in life...

"I am much more than what the world perceives me as. As a disabled person or a woman, I can create something beautiful like Fruit Chaat. I can take care of every relationship."

My name is Tanzila Khan; I hail from and currently reside in Lahore in Pakistan. My journey began on 14th October 1990 in a city called Sialkot in Pakistan. My father was posted there whilst serving in the Pakistan Army. I have an older brother, and I have been told that my birth was looked forward to with great anticipation by my parents. In those days, nearly 30 years ago, getting the gender of a child checked in Pakistan was not an option, but my mother said that her intuition told her that she would have a baby girl. As a result, she did a lot of shopping for a girl, and when I was born and she took me home, she took great pride in dressing me in the girl's clothes she had brought.

My parents welcomed me with open arms, and my birth was a time of great rejoicing for them. From there on, my birthday was celebrated yearly, with a lot of pomp and happiness. Having said that, I can imagine the shock my parents must have felt and how difficult it must have been for them when they realised that their daughter had a disability, especially in a society where women go through different layers of judgement. The layers vary, and you can be judged on your gender, being a woman, the colour of your skin, your body type, and even your features. My legs were deformed below my knees; although I had feet, they were inverted. I could wear shoes, but I couldn't walk, and my disability was quite visible. It was never a hindrance, and as I grew up, I enjoyed life as any healthy person did.

Ever since my parents brought me home, my life has been amazing – challenging, yes, with many emotions that have shaped and changed me. I was the apple of my parents' eye; hence, I was pampered a lot. My brother was just two years older than me, but how he looked after me and supported me; I consider myself very lucky to have him in my life!

Until I was seven years old, because my father was in the army, we moved around quite a bit, with him being posted to different parts of Pakistan every two to three years. Besides being in the army, my father also belonged to a landowning family, and my mother comes from a large family. Consequently, I had many cousins to play with as I grew up. Furthermore, I was well accepted, and my disability never created any issues.

At a young age, I realised that I couldn't move to do certain tasks or activities, like playing games, so I put my energy into allocating tasks to others and became very good at it. Just to cite an example, if we were playing a game of Seven Stones or Hide n Seek – even though I couldn't move around and directly become part of the game, I would take charge, and I would be assigning tasks to other members, telling them to hide either here or there or to do this or that. If we were playing games that involved running, lovingly, my cousins would pick me up and run.

Regardless of my disability, I would be involved in every game or activity. We also had a village near my maternal grandmother, and we would visit there often. I remember it was a time filled with fun and games in the village, playing around trees, going into the fields, talking to the villagers, cooking in small pots or on a makeshift stove, picking sugarcane and oranges ourselves and trips to the tube well. That was my beautiful, enriching reality! It was these natural surroundings that allowed me to enjoy and respect nature. My fondest memories are of green fields and being attacked by cows. At that age, I thought that was the worst thing that could happen. Life had other plans; it was like life was saying, "hold on honey". Being attacked by cows is nothing compared to what life throws at you. To say the least, my childhood was blissful.

When I started school, my parents opted to send me to a regular mainstream school and refused to send me to a *'disabled-oriented special school'.* I'm not implying that special schools are not good enough; over the years, many special schools in Pakistan have been established for differently abled children and young people, but these schools and institutions need a lot more resources, teacher training, technology, and attention. When you go to a regular school, you can understand how the world works, your presence and position in it, and where you fit in mainstream society. There is one major issue; however, in Pakistan, disabled children are usually refused admission to mainstream schools, which are designed for so-called average, non-disabled children.

Luckily, my parents didn't face any issues with my admission to Beaconhouse school (a private school) for my early education in Rahim Yar Khan, Pakistan, where my father was posted at that time. On the contrary, the school was very happy to have me. Their only concern was accommodating me in the right way – my parents took the initiative; they went to meet the floor management and explain things to them, and they were told not to worry. Schools tend to get concerned if there is a problem, for, they don't want to be singled out and receive bad publicity. My parents took the responsibility and did everything to facilitate the school administration, which was a big deal. In retrospect, when I think of it, it could have been due to my father being a landowner and an army officer, that his influence played a part in securing my admission.

After the initial years, we found a permanent home in Lahore, where my mother settled with my brother and me, while my father continued to move around for his postings. This decision was taken so that my education was not disturbed. For me, getting admission to a mainstream school was just winning 10 % of the battle as there were several issues regarding my access and resources. At times, my wheelchair could not access the toilets or the laboratories; sometimes, I could not make my way to the canteen to get water. To say the least, the school infrastructure was not built to accommodate my needs; and hence, we had to change schools a few times. Barrier-free access is significant, if children with disabilities are to be included in mainstream in Pakistan and indeed, in third-world countries. The challenges I faced in some of the private schools in urban areas of Pakistan, are just the tip of the iceberg.

I had some movement in my legs, but I couldn't stand on them; besides that, I was physically very active. My parents would always hire a nanny for me to manage my daily chores and accompany me to school. I was very tiny as a baby and was nearly 4 years old when I started attending school. So, I was carried around in elementary school by my nanny to class, then to the playground or the bathroom. At that young age, I could not use crutches or a wheelchair as my disability was such that my legs were bent – they couldn't be moved to become longer.

At a very young age, I became very conscious of my body; I understood my position and the attention I was getting.

Back then, I was very social; I would easily make friends and throw parties at my house unannounced. My family would not know – all my friends would show up at my home; I gave my family a fright with my surprise parties! At the age of seven, my father took a one year's leave from the army and decided to take me to the U.S.A. for medical treatment. He explored various doctors and medical treatments offered in the U.S. for my disability and was given a lot of hope regarding it. His desire was to see me walk and have a stable life, or else the world would not be an easy place to live in. I admire his courage, motivation and long-term vision to strive ahead – even though, at the time, there were financial issues with land and other issues in the family. After consultation with a few doctors, my father decided on a paediatric orthopaedic surgeon from Valley Hospital in New Jersey, who he thought would give me the chance to walk.

Obtaining a U.S. visa is another tale in itself! Back in the 1990s, this was a cumbersome and difficult process. The officials at the American Embassy weren't easy on my father; they would ask difficult questions, such as *"why do you have to go?"*, *"why can't you get treatment here in Pakistan?"*, *"there is no need"*, etc. At that time, we were posted in Lahore, so we had to travel to Islamabad every now and then for our visa appointments. Our visas were rejected a couple of times, but my father put in a lot of effort, and finally, he and I were issued with one.

On the other hand, my mother and brother's visas were rejected – we were shocked. Since I was just seven, my father was annoyed; he tried to make them understand how young I was. Since I was just seven my father was angry at the Embassy and tried to make them understand that, because I was going to America for treatment, I needed my mother with me. The embassy refused to grant my mother and brother a visa. With this being the case, my father decided to take me to America on his own.

It was a huge undertaking, but we managed, and once we were there, we bonded so well and agreed that life was about being happy, living and exploring! We were a great duo. We travelled across the U.S, went to Disneyland and Las Vegas, and had a great time.

The only probable solution, according to the doctors in my case, was to perform surgery. Through this surgery, a small part of my leg would be amputated, because it wasn't required to be used. This part was my fibula. I only had a fibula and not a tibia; the stronger bone. I don't know how he did it, but a day before my surgery, my father managed to fly my mother and my brother to be with me. God is so kind and full of miracles. I was overjoyed to see my mother and brother at my bedside and for some reason, the entire experience of my operation was delightful; it wasn't daunting. Everyone around me was so nice.

The late 90s in America was very different. They didn't care that I was Muslim, Asian or brown – for them, I was Tanzila, a cute girl who talked a lot, and they just wanted to be friends with me. One lasting memory that stayed with me from this trip was the way my brother looked after me.

While we were in the U.S, we lived in a place where there were children from other countries. I would be playing with them, and once when I was playing, they started bullying me, and I began to cry. At that point, my brother took me aside and said, *"Tanzila, learn to speak for yourself; if they are bullying you, learn to respond!"*. That was the first time I stood up for myself – before that, I always thought that I wasn't supposed to say anything, because these kids were my friends. I guess this was a turning point; ever since, no one has been able to walk all over me. My brother nudged me in this direction... he's like a third parent to me, and he will always be like that.

After surgery, whenever I went for therapy or had my wounds tended to, my very loving nurses would take me on a round of the hospital in a wheelchair and tell everybody that I was their favourite patient. I really loved them; they taught me lessons in humanity, empathy and kindness.

After the healing period was over, we were introduced to the world of prosthetics, which was all very new to me and my family. The plan was to get a prosthetic after my surgery. I got prosthetics done on both legs and with the help of therapy I was able to stand up and walk as well. It was a very emotional moment for me and my family when I took the first steps. I was able to stand and walk, but as to be expected, this feat was achieved with great difficulty. Learning to walk for me was like learning a new sport – not easy. In a way my father's dream was coming true, he had strived so hard to get me to this stage in life where I was able to take a few steps...it was an uphill task, but I was trying to manage. I don't know how to put it; if it's destiny... I did start walking in the U.S, I would walk around, although with great difficulty, but it is commendable the support that I had on this journey. I was never alone in my struggle as I was duly supported by my family and the medical staff.

After the initial rehabilitation phase, I was getting better, and it was time to come back home. Once we were back, everything had changed for me. When I started going to school, I would walk with the help of a walker; it would take me a long time, and I would usually arrive late. It created a spectacle, and I was not used to it. So as an easy way out, I started using my wheelchair instead. This led me to not walk, so the entire goal of walking disappeared, and I got busy with my education as my father got busy with his job, and my mother and brother got busy with theirs. So, the entire aim of the operation in America took a backseat, eventually fading into the background.

Of course, the experience was there – my father kept urging me to continue walking and put in an effort. I used to keep telling him that I would do so next week, but next week never came. I felt the environment wasn't suitable for me to walk and I didn't want to become a spectacle. I think not being in a wheelchair was a spectacle as opposed to being in a wheelchair, which is a bit more common in Pakistan as you see people in wheelchairs around you. My gait was never straight, so walking in a crooked way affected me negatively. Also, I had just started my periods. It was a time of self-realisation of how my body was growing and changing. I was becoming more conscious of my physical self and walking in a crooked way and drawing attention to myself, was never an option. People might think that I was quite young, but even at that young age, my self-awareness was strong.

I was somebody who, as a teenager, was very conscious of the way I looked. I celebrated every feature of my body. My teen years were amazing and when I was in school, I got red streaks done in my hair! I wasn't a good student. In fact, the teachers were fed up with me and kept reminding me that the future would be bleak, if I did not study. My interests were elsewhere. I was always more interested in extracurricular activities and recess periods. I was more into talking about movies, books and actors, about living, but not academic work. I fully participated in extracurricular activities, debates, public speaking, and art competitions. I represented my school at different events and was not interested in attending school. I had very good friends – it's shocking that even at that young age, there were eleven of us sitting together and if there was an activity that I couldn't participate in, all eleven of us would refuse to participate in it.

The camaraderie was amazing even though there were a lot of friendships that ended, and of course, there were fights. These are everyday experiences, and we would fight over different ideas and disagree with each other, but at the same time, there was a very strong bond between us and especially me, as my friends were always empathetic towards my needs, which never ceased to amaze me. Some of them did believe that I got undue attention, while on the other hand, many loved and appreciated me for who I was, and we enjoyed each other's company. I was always popular in my school among the juniors and the seniors. I was the campaigner everybody knew, and I knew everybody.

When I was in my mid-teens, right after I started my periods, I realised my identity as a person with a disability was too fluff. It's very charitable; people love and know me, but I still wanted to become someone. Someone who had a lot more to offer. I always loved to read, and I loved to write as well. It was then that I started to write, wrote a few poems, and finally, decided to write my own book. I wrote a book because I wanted to be known as an *"Author"* and not as the *"girl in the wheelchair"*. *A Story of Mexico* is based on the fantasy about this beautiful place called Mexico, which I had never visited, but my imagination made me write about it. Yes, my book came out while I was still in school. A prominent television network invited me to come on one of its shows and talk about my book. It was when the mainstream media was predominant, and the social media frenzy did not exist.

I used my attention positively by drawing awareness to important issues. I spoke less about my life and more about other people's problems. I bluntly told the media that it is biased and that it needs help, which is why I wanted to be a part of it. Due to this attention, I became a young leader and a spokesperson for many different causes. As a result, I became this mini celebrity overnight, and my identity changed. I received respect and recognition as someone who is now a contributor to literature and is known as an author, instead of the disabled girl in the wheelchair!

After the release of my first book, I received a lot of attention, and my grades started to fall. As a result, my teachers got together, formed a group and urged the principal to stop my registration for the Cambridge 'O' level exams. My teachers had simply given up on me; they thought that I would not be able to score good grades and that this would bring a bad name to the school. Students scoring As and A stars was a big deal and a matter of prestige, so if there was a C or a D, that would be like heartache. I, in turn, pleaded with the principal to give me one last chance, which she did on the promise that I would put in 100% effort. While I was in her office, she pointed to a tree outside and said, *"Tanzila do you see the tree outside?"*. I said, *"yes"* and then she said, *"I will tie you to that tree; if you score anything less than a B – you must score either Bs or As".* I took a sigh of relief and said that *"I will!"*. I asked her to write something for me, and she wrote on a sticky note, *"You can do it"* - Rubina Anjum.

This was when I started working very hard, because my aim was to gain the respect of someone that I admired. After my O-level exams, during the summertime, I started an internship at SOS - Village with orphan children. When I got my result, I got two As and all the rest Bs. I was absolutely delighted. In hindsight, I wasn't motivated enough in the beginning, but the conversation between myself and the principal was the turning point; I called my parents, and they were very happy and took a big cake to the school, and my principal was delighted. I told her, *"Mam, the tree sacrifice, had to be saved!"*.

Afterwards, my A-levels were terrible; I was going through many personal and emotional issues at the time. I was exposed to the real world and had started getting a lot of attention from the opposite sex. I don't know why; even though I used a wheelchair, people would still want to be around me and send gifts, ask for my phone number and pass me theirs. I would be asked questions such as, *"Which college do you attend?"* and I had to tell them that I was still in school. I was too young to choose and still had the world to explore. I enjoyed the interaction of talking to people, especially the opposite sex. I learnt a lot about how men think, how to speak to them, and how to keep my grace and dignity. It taught me how not to let my emotions get the better of me. I always thought that, as a disabled woman, I would miss out on many things, but I haven't – I'm blessed!

In my own way, I would flaunt my achievements, intellect, and body. It would be more like, *"I'm a published author; who are you? you're just an A-level student"*. I already knew that, looks-wise, I had been blessed with a beautiful face; I just wanted to ensure that my personality stood out more.

When I turned 17, I became extremely religious. I started studying the Holy Quran. What triggered me toward religion? As far as I can recall, I think I fell in love with Allah – the one and only God in Islam. I really started feeling his presence in my surroundings and how people would behave with me. I started reading a lot about Sufism and the conversations I had with Allah. Believe me, I never blamed Allah for my disability; in fact, I have always taken my disability as a blessing – always!

Even if I felt low, it was because of a reason, an incident or an emotion, but never my disability. Having said that, I discovered Allah's love and I just wanted to please Him. I became very religious I would fast here and there, read the Holy Quran, and pray with my prayer beads - tasbih.

One day, I was fasting, and I woke up around 10:00 am and couldn't move from my bed. I don't know what happened; I felt immense pain in my lower back and leg, and I couldn't move. My family thought it was probably a sprain or something, and it would get better with a bit of movement. Lo and behold, a week had passed, but my pain continued, so much so that I could not go to the toilet and relieve myself. I could not say my daily prayers – it was the wrong time. I was in so much pain that no one could touch me; even if someone sat on the bed, it would hurt me. If someone sat next to me and laughed, it would hurt me, and I would scream with pain. We could not diagnose the problem; it got so bad that one-day an ambulance had to be called to take me to the hospital.

At the hospital, they diagnosed a rare infection in my backbone. I was in various hospitals in Lahore for three months. During these months, my body was infused with strange antibiotics, making it a depository of antibiotics and having all kinds of side effects. It was just so crazy, and I kept thinking, *"Allah, I was trying to please you; what are you doing to me? Don't you love me? Don't you like me anymore? What's happening?"*. I had become religious, and then this episode happened, and I thought, *"am I being tested by Allah? Do I go astray or remain steadfast?"*. I was so confused. My three-month illness was undefinable; we did not know if it was permanent or cancer, but thank Allah it was not cancer.

I don't know. Allah knows! But I'm sure those three months were a test for me! It was a very difficult time for not just me, but my entire family – our lives had stopped. It was worse than my disability – I had learnt to live with my disability! Then one day, suddenly, I was fine! Allah made me go through this whole process of humility. It taught me many things about myself and how dependent I am on his mercy. It was a constant spiritual awakening journey that I was going through...but Allah had a beautiful plan. My 18th birthday occurred during those three months, and I celebrated it on the ward. I also wrote my second book during this period. It is about a teenager who is growing up in Pakistan and is facing the difficulty of settling between the eastern and western world. It was called *"The Perfect Situation"*. After two months of recovery, I went back to school.

I was doing my A-Levels when Allah invited my family and

me for the holy pilgrimage of Hajj. Hajj is a pilgrimage made to the Kaaba, the "House of Allah", in the sacred city of Makkah in Saudi Arabia, which every adult Muslim must complete at least once in their lifetime, if they are physically and financially able to do so. The entire experience of being able to do Tawaf on my own in a manual wheelchair was amazing. Tawaf is one of the principal rites of the pilgrimage and refers to walking in circles around the Kaaba in an anti- clockwise motion. Seven complete circuits, each starting and ending at the Hajar al-Aswad, the Black Stone, the sacred rock encased with silver and placed in the south-eastern corner of the Kaaba, which is believed to have descended from heaven, constitute one Tawaf.

In contrast, I was sick just a few months before the Hajj, and to have so much energy to do seven rounds of Tawaf of The Holy Kaaba in a manual wheelchair, was remarkable! That entire experience blew me away. I realised that Allah had an amazing plan for me, and the three-month ordeal was preparation. It was there, in front of the Holy Kaaba, I pledged to Allah to cover my head – do the hijab as a sign of dedication, as a sign of acceptance of my identity as a Muslim woman. I have loved it and have never taken it off; it's now been twelve years.

Ironically things suddenly changed after I started wearing the hijab. Before, I used to attract attention, especially from the opposite sex. Now, I had become the *"sister"* to everybody, to be greeted with Salaam – meaning peace be upon you. Even though I am the same person, it was like saying, *"what's wrong with all of you?"* – men respect you if you're covered.

Life did not stop there. My experiences went ahead of me. During my A-levels, I started an organisation called *'Creative Alley,'* a venture that held simulations and workshops for community empowerment, especially for the youth. I was born with a disability, and being a female, I knew that life can be hard, but I also knew how much life can give back to you, if you decide to give yourself to life. The idea behind starting this organisation was that I am alive and kicking against all odds, and since I am here, why not make some good change while still dancing through life. It is my way of giving back to the community/youth. We started smaller initiatives, such as theatre, workshops etc.

Through *Creative Alley*, I got attention from other countries, such as India and when I was twenty-one, I was invited to participate in a youth activism summit in Delhi. Since that day, I haven't looked back. I started travelling that same year and went to Sri Lanka and many other countries. I came back and expanded Creative Alley across Pakistan, and we won a lot of grants. I met so many amazing people; I represented my identity, culture and religion on many platforms. I met royalty and celebrities and won competitions, and my profile has been expanding ever since.

Currently, I run a start-up business, *"Girlythings. pk"*. We deliver feminine hygiene products to women all over Pakistan, and I fund it through my savings. Recently, I have been approached by an international civil rights organisation in recognition of my work. They were impressed with the model of my business and wanted to know more about it. Hard work does get recognised! In addition to *Girlythings*, I consult a lot on soft skills training for the corporate sector. I charge a high fee, but I offer good original content, and I don't sell pity. I'm more about soft skills development, and motivation is a by-product of every training event. I like to train young people and prepare them for life, conflicts, communication, etc., to help them develop some sense of delivery.

I have undergone several training courses and fellowships, and during those fellowships, I have never been shy to learn and develop my skills more. Even today, I take a lot of courses on Udemy (an online learning resource). Whenever I travel - I sign up for training. I develop my content for the training to make it relatable to one's culture and context. I believe training should be contextually relevant to engage the participants and make the material easy to implement and understand. For this reason, I quote Rumi, a spiritual mystic and Ashfaque Ahmed a well-known inspirational writer in Pakistan. I seldom quote Steve Jobs or Elon Musk – they haven't been colonised and don't know our language!

When I do youth training with corporate entities, I relate it to inclusion, diversity and gender, to name a few. For a lot of training on communication, writing skills, event management, community building, projects and entrepreneurship, I like to use theatre, for it helps me to shed light on many taboos in our society.

I am also into motivational speaking. Over the years, I have become an International Motivational Speaker and have delivered and worked on four continents across the globe. Through these consultancies and speaking engagements, I try and fund the community projects I'm involved in, on disability, women's empowerment, education and the environment. I certainly feel very blessed and privileged to be able to share and have an impact on others in similar situations.

I have worked for almost every cause in the world, but only recently have I started to work for disability rights. I recently produced a short film called "Fruit Chaat" (an Urdu word which means a bowl of fruit mix). I wrote, produced and acted in it, while my friend Moiz Abbas directed it. The birth of Fruit Chaat was something that came out of this nasty comment, *"disabled people use their disability as a get-away by playing the sympathy card to get a lot of opportunities in life".* The film is a comedy and highlights the hopes of a newly minted yet disabled graduate girl in Pakistan looking for opportunities. It explores all the limitations that society places on her, and all this is encapsulated in a funny, heart- warming story. Fruit Chaat (fruit dish) happens to be a very cultural thing in Pakistan, having a typical flavour and colour. That is exactly what the central character of Shabana (played by me) is implying, *"I am much more than what the world perceives me as. As a disabled person or a woman, I can create something beautiful like Fruit Chaat. I can take care of every relationship".*

Shabana represents a very important segment of society, especially women with disabilities. To be precise, it was essential to highlight what a woman with such disabilities can go through in life in Pakistan and in South Asian countries. She has the same desires and wishes as any normal girl, and her disabilities amplify her experience. Still, I don't make her an odd one out. I have drawn her character from my own life, and she is a happy and empowered character. I wanted to convey the message that Shabana can not only sell fruits, but also, make good Fruit Chaat and do several other tasks just like a normal person, ensuring that her disability does not come in between her dreams.

In Fruit Chaat I want people to know that:

- People with disability want to do things the right way.
- It is society that stereotypes them.
- Society expects them to be a certain way and then exploits and typecasts them.

Fruit Chaat started with a lot of thought and a lot of mental effort went into it, to ensure that the correct language was used; to get the message across.
The film also deals with the idea of women's empowerment. I think the first thing we need to do is humanise women, give them the due credit for their contributions, and then the empowerment will sprout out in its own way. A woman has the same ambitions and dreams as a man, and she should seek the same respect for whatever work she does. It could be housework,

being a great mother at home, or being a good boss in the office. Just allow women to be themselves, and that is what I think is empowerment. Recently, 'Fruit Chaat' secured third place in the awards announced by ZEE5 Global, the largest OTT platform for South Asian Content (https://dailytodaysmuslim.com/zee5-global-winner-fruit- chat). The short film was very much liked, and thought is being given to turning it into a web series.

I'm currently completing my third book, a collection of interesting short stories. My work has helped me develop so much positivity that, most of the time, I feel a halo of happiness and contentment around me. I am always in a festive mood; it doesn't matter if I am with two or one hundred people. The satisfaction, attention, network, recognition and the respect I get through my work have been amazing; we mentor and support each other – it's beautiful.

I like to make sure that my presence speaks in a community or event – it is like branding in its own way. It's a representation of a mindset; I make sure that it is documented and well- received – It is a representation of a community; when Tanzila walks into a room, she is not pitied; she is respected. People reach out to her because they know she has value to add. The next time they meet a person with a disability, they see that they must give them equal respect – whether on the street or elsewhere. When I see a disabled person as a beggar, I know that person as a "self-employed" person. My goal in life is to make sure that these profiles are well respected. So, the whole idea of not looking at people with disabilities as mere "beneficiaries"; I really want to eliminate this mindset. In my work, I have been an executor of projects – my beneficiaries were very much able-bodied running, jogging people. I was working for them; I was getting funding for them. So, all the time, the stereotyping of making a person look like they need help. It's high time; it needs to change!

Choosing a partner to celebrate life with me is very important, and I want to take my time to make that choice. Right now, I'm very excited to be single, travel and do more projects on my own. I really enjoy my own company and solitude. Later, when the timing is right, I want to scan around and look for the best option and settle down. Plan "B", if I don't find anybody as crazy as me, I'll adopt children and continue the amazing life I have. I want to become a mother, whether I give birth or not. Walking in the past has never been a priority for me, but it's funny that today it is a priority. Today, I have taken up the challenge upon myself; I want to give it a shot. I have this feeling that just because I'm 30 years old doesn't mean I can't do it. If I put effort into it, I will achieve it!

Lastly, I want to change the idea that anybody can be a leader; they can come from anywhere. Any person could be one, a child or an older person. There isn't a specific profile that dictates what a "leader" looks like. Leadership speaks. They are in our homes, on the streets; it's a lifestyle; anybody could have it. Being physically able or disabled has nothing to do with it; it is the mindset that makes us reach our goals in life.

Uzma's story

The accident took away my legs, but it gave me something in return. I never stopped believing in myself; I never gave up.

I would ask myself, 'Why can't they see that I have worth? Why is my work always measured against my disability?

Although I was born in Faisalabad, when I was six years old, we moved to Karachi as my father got a job in the government. My upbringing in the metropolitan city of Karachi changed my perspective of city life. Karachi is the capital of the Pakistani province of Sindh, and it is located on the coast of the Arabian sea. It is the largest city in Pakistan and the seventh largest in the world. The best thing about Karachi is that it never sleeps; you will find ice cream and pizzas at any time of the night.

In 2003, my father resigned from his government job and set up his own business. My mother, as a housewife, dedicated her life to ensuring that her four children were well fed, were well kept and got the best education she and my father could afford. I am the eldest of four siblings, with a brother who is followed by two more sisters. We are a very close-knit loving family and have always had a strong bond between us.

Before 2003, I had a very active student life. I was ambitious, bold, and competitive. I would participate in all sorts of sports and debate competitions. I would go out and eat with friends and despite my family being traditional, they trusted me. I was full of life, full of dreams, was someone who would one day conquer the world with her energy, spirit and grit, but life had other plans. It always does!

In 2003, I was in the fourth semester, enrolled on a distance learning programme at an international university for my bachelor's degree in software engineering. One Sunday on a fine winter's day, I left with my friends to take tuition classes. We were four of us in the car and all I remember is, or what I was told, that the car skid and fell from an elevated road and was hit by the oncoming traffic. Passers-by took me out of the car, in fact, pulled me from the vehicle. I am sure they mishandled me in their desire to help someone who was losing a lot of blood and would soon die. How can they be blamed? No one is ready or trained for such situations.

The last thing I remember when I was taken to hospital was that I could not feel anything below my abdomen, and I asked the doctors to anaesthetise me because of the pain. The medical staff on duty could not ascertain my injury and did not know what to do. By the time my family arrived, two hours had already passed. Realising that the hospital I was taken to would only further complicate my case, my family moved me to Liaquat National Hospital (LNH), the largest private-sector care hospital in Karachi. It was now six hours since my accident and when I reached the hospital, I was unconscious.

Initially, the doctors who attended to me first at LNH were not hopeful of my survival. I was told later that when they took me to LNH, the emergency doctor that night on duty told my mother, *"She will not survive!"*. You know mothers are mothers, and they can stomp on paradise. She replied, *"you are not God"*.

More than 14 hours after my accident, the doctors decided to operate. My spine was broken in two. The surgeon later told me they took the blood out from my backbone and fixed it by inserting a nail. Low chances of survival. But hey, I can now show you my spine x-rays, which clearly show the pin that holds my spine together.

In 2003, after 23 years, my life ended, and now my journey started from intensive care units to high dependency units, to a private room in a hospital. It soon dawned on my family and me that due to my spinal cord injury, I was now a paraplegic. None of us at that time had the slightest idea of what is paraplegia. Paraplegia is an impairment in motor or sensory function of the lower extremities. It is usually caused by spinal cord injury or a congenital condition that affects the spinal canal's neural (brain) elements. With this, you can't move your legs, and the lower abdomen also does not work. In the beginning, even simple movements like turning and sitting could not be done without assistance. I later learned that the time lapse between the accident and the surgery had significant consequences as my present condition could have been avoided with timely medical intervention.

After staying in the hospital for more than one and a half months, my injury affected my organs. Firstly, my lungs started to retain water, which had to be drained, which is a procedure that caused me immense pain. As the focus was on my backbone, my complaints of pain in my arms were ignored, but after one month, an x-ray showed that the cause of the pain was a broken bone. I had to undergo surgery, and the bone had to be broken again and then fixed as it had been joined incorrectly. Believe me, that pain was worse than the backbone pain. The reason was because I had been given a great deal of anaesthetic during the backbone surgery, and I could only be given a little this time. The lack of sufficient anaesthetic meant that I was conscious throughout the operation. The pain was so excruciating that I cannot explain it with words!! Oh, it was unimaginable…. even now, when I think about it, it gives me goosebumps. After surgery, my arm took nearly six months to heal and become fully functional.

You cannot imagine the unbearable pain I went through when they made me sit for the first time, although it was done with a jacket, an aid used by people with spinal cord injuries to give them some mobility. As I was given a lot of anaesthesia, I was primarily numb and couldn't understand much, making it difficult to think straight. One day my university teachers came to see me, and I tried to get up, but I could not. That was when I realise that my leg was not moving, that I would never walk again; or leave my bed again. It was a big jolt!

Not only had I lost the function of my legs, but the ability to control my urination, and I would wear diapers all my life. I would never play sports and would never go to university. I would never be able to marry, and I had nothing but a dead- end in front of me. My wings were clipped, and I was put in a cage. These were the thoughts surrounding me at the time.

At this point, I was still in the HDU, and all my relatives and friends used to be around me, and everybody would give their opinions. You know how Pakistani society works. I could hear comments like, *"she has met with this accident during her full youth...what will happen with her, what will happen to her parents, what were the sins of her parents?"*. These were friends, relatives, outsiders, and all kinds of people passing their verdict on my accident. They did not realise that my family and I did not need their insensitive comments. We were under tremendous psychological and financial strain. For example, my father was out of a job and in a start-up. My brother had to leave his school for A-level exams.

My sisters missed their exams as no one was there to take them to school and to pick them up. The hospital bill was climbing like Elon Musk's rockets.

However, some people offered wise words. They would motivate me. *"You are doing well; it doesn't matter if Allah has put you into this, he will also take you out from this; there must be some reason"*. There was an uncle who was my father's friend; he told me. *"What was bound to happen has happened, and it was your destiny.... you'll have to sort it out and figure it out yourself but don't cry in front of your parents ever!"*. That conversation really hit me!!! Until now, whenever I face a problem, I never tell my parents. Also, I knew I had to restrain myself and not cry, especially in front of my mother, to whom I'm very attached emotionally. I knew that if I lost it, she would too. She had such firm faith in Allah (the one and only God in Islam) that she came to me and said, *"everything will be okay"*. To say the least, I was surrounded by my family and good friends as well, which helped me endure this ordeal with a smile.

I was in my twenties at the time of the accident and was a final-year student, but when it came to the prognosis of my condition, the doctors did not communicate this directly to me. When I gained consciousness in ICU, the doctor who did the operation came to me and said, *"everything is okay; we'll shift you to the HDU in a couple of days"*. This was a senior surgeon, and I understood that seeing my condition, he had to comfort me, which he did and did not say anything else.

During my hospital stay, none of the doctors spoke to me directly about my condition to prepare me for what was to come. Afterwards, I realised that, in Pakistan, this is a very cultural thing; doctors do not talk directly to their patients and explain; instead, they share it with their family members. This is a significant gap in doctor-patient relations that needs to be bridged. Now in retrospect, I think this conversation could have prepared my family and me better, and many mishaps I experienced could have easily been avoided.

After all the pain I went through, when I first sat in a wheelchair, that was the moment when I realised this was it!!! It was tough, no doubt about it!! It was not just the physical trauma I was already facing, for the psychological one was more engulfing, with the thought that this chair will be my lifelong companion! This feeling of despair was short-term as I had my faith, and I thank Allah he gave me the courage to get through all of this. Slowly and gradually, I adjusted to the situation, tried to do everything with my siblings, played, laughed, and gave the sense that everything was normal. It was not easy, believe me, and if it were not for my faith in Allah and the support of my loved ones, I would not have had the courage to accept my disability wholeheartedly.

Another person besides my parents and my siblings, who I drew strength from, was my Mamu (my maternal uncle). He was a tower of strength for me, and I always drew inspiration from him. He always had a very positive impact on me with his support and encouragement and this continued even after my accident. After my accident, he celebrated my birthday with a large birthday celebration. He was the other superhero besides my parents and my dear beloved siblings. Without these real superheroes, I would not have been able to even take another step forward towards my rehabilitation. They are the ones who helped me accept this reality and take it as a challenge.

As time passed, I realised that there are a lot of other problems surrounding a person with paraplegia. Since we were not guided through the pros and cons of my condition, we are thrown in at the deep end. It was as if someone had opened a pandora's box. I had to swim without knowing how to. We had to learn everything through trial and error and self-research.

When you are paraplegic, you lose bladder control, so I had a urine catheter for 1 year. As for stools, it was the bedpan, and at home, it was my brother who had to lift me from the wheelchair to the toilet seat and vice versa. As luck would have it, I had developed bed sores because of our lack of knowledge about my condition. They are considered one of the significant problems with paraplegia; if you get them, healing them is the biggest challenge in the world. At that time, my youngest sister was studying law and had her final exams. I remember the doctor told us not to let me stay wet at night as I could not go to the washroom alone. So, when I would call my sister at 2 am in the morning, she would come and help me and take me to the toilet. For passing stools, my brother would be doing the transfer. For two years, I could not go to the bathroom by myself. We kept researching on the internet to find a solution to this problem, and we came across a type of washroom chair used by people with paraplegia to facilitate their toilet needs. I had it ordered from abroad, and by acquiring it, I got a bit independent, at least with my toilet needs.

I strongly feel that, if a person goes through something like what I went through, it's the responsibility of the doctors and the medical staff to guide the patient not only about the condition, but also the future challenges and possible solutions to those problems. This lack of knowledge also resulted in a delayed start to my physiotherapy, which proved to be quite ineffective as my muscle tone had started to deteriorate. Most importantly, the equipment and resources needed for therapy and rehabilitation for a patient like me were not available then, even in the best private medical facilities in Karachi.

I was an ordinary fun-loving girl in her early twenties enjoying life, and this one accident had changed my life forever. My perspective towards life, thoughts, dreams and desires had taken a complete turn. In the first 3 years after my accident, I could not even get up alone. I could not sit on the bed. My brother would help transfer me from the bed to the wheelchair, from the wheelchair to the toilet, pick me up and put me in the car. In those days, we lived in a penthouse apartment on the 5th floor, so if sometimes the elevator was not working, the poor guy would pick me up and take me up the stairs one flight at a time. Can you imagine how much effort it took? Thankfully, I also received strong physical and emotional support. I considered myself blessed indeed, and I am sure my brother also did it to keep fit and to develop a muscular physique.

It took me three years to get out of bed and into a wheelchair without feeling nauseous or dizzy. Despite my family and the support I had around me, we had our dark days. The frustrations would creep in. I would lose hope some days. My sister would not get enough sleep as I had to wake her up 2 or 3 times every night. My mother would feel depressed, and my father felt the financial strain. We would self-destruct, but we always rebounded stronger. The trauma was not just physical; it was more psychological and managing it all and putting up a brave front took a lot of courage. Hence, I took the plunge and dived right into my studies. I started studying from home, passed my exams and got my degree in software engineering.

Life finally started to do its magic, heal! and my father took us to Syria, my first international trip after the accident. We visited the shrine of Bibi Zainab. She was the granddaughter of Prophet Muhammad (peace be upon him). Seeing her shrine, I realised that even when she lost her brothers and sons, she fought back more strongly. If I thought of being her follower in my heart, I knew I had to fight back. I did not look back after that.

Honestly, my disability never proved to be a deterrent from enjoying ourselves as a family. We would go around enjoying ourselves in the city and taking trips abroad as we used to do before my accident. I received the family's same unconditional support during these foreign travels. Of course, it was always prior planning to selecting destinations offering maximum facilities and barrier-free access for the disabled. As usual, my brother would carry me up, if there were stairs on these trips and no elevators. At the time of my accident, I was in my early twenties, unmarried, a student, and so were my siblings, who did a lot for me, and the bond grew more robust as time passed.

As students do, after completing their studies, I also started applying for jobs. I guess I was naïve; I expected just as my family and I had accepted my disability and learnt to live with it, others would too. No, I was wrong! I was in for another reality check. The dynamics had changed now that I was a wheelchair user, which is a taboo in our society, so nobody wanted to hire me. Ironically, I was never even asked to come in for an interview; it was never a matter of discussion. I was just refused point blank!! After many attempts and no luck, before disappointment engulfed me, I thought of doing my Master's. Believe me, I applied to every college/ university offering programmes I was interested in, but I was refused. Most refusals were based on the reasoning that they could not provide me with barrier-free access, which entailed having ramps around the building and arranging classes on the ground floor. Although if you just think about it, there were not many adjustments that this would have involved.

We can say that society is just scared of being associated with disabled people. A few years later, I came to know from a reliable source that when I was applying for my Master's, a renowned university had instructed the interviewers to fail any disabled applicant in the interview process. I guess the most important factor here to note is the attitude and the mindset of the school/ college management, employers, and organisations. Luckily, I had also applied to do my master's at the Pakistan Air force - Karachi Institute of Information Technology (PAF-KIET) in computer science. My admission was accepted, which made me heave a sigh of relief. Surprisingly, these people were very supportive, and they arranged the classes on the ground floor only to facilitate me.

I had to face the outside world, knowing that they would judge me in their hearts, that my spine broke because of my sin, my family's sins, and the wrath of God. I was judged every day. I was the outcast. I was the witch who was to be burnt. Little did they know, I was burnt every day by the judgement. The accident took away my legs, but it gave me something in return. I never stopped believing in myself; I never gave up.

After my Master's degree, I again started applying for jobs and faced the same taboos, same barriers, hurdles, closed doors, questions and to some extent, the same wrong assumptions. *"How will you do it? How will you sit, etc.?"*. The main thing that bothered me was that no one was willing to allow me to discuss my situation and what I could and could not do. They were not seeing beyond my disability! This kind of behaviour made me think, *"Okay, fine, don't trust me, but trust your ability to hire someone and adjust?"*. If the person cannot do it, they will just leave themselves, but people do not have this sense.

Nearly five years had passed since my accident, and I continued to plough on whatever way I thought was appropriate. So, one day my younger sister came back from university with some of her friends, and she said, *"the 3rd of December is coming, it is the international day of the disabled, and we are planning to visit a non-governmental organisation for disabled people, do you have any ideas for this day?"*. Hearing this request triggered something in me, and I completely lost my temper. I think these were the pent-up emotions, the frustrations, the setbacks that had been piling up over all these years. I just flared up and said, *"there are no facilities for the disabled, no infrastructure, no study or job options and on this day, visiting a few NGOs with high-profile people. What are you trying to achieve? Disabled does not just need empathy; they need more"*. After I had vented out these feelings and calmed myself down, I started to think hard about how I could capitalise on this day. Suddenly the idea of holding a press conference came to my mind. My father, my anchor, was the first person I shared the idea with; he liked it and gave me the go-ahead.

Corresponding with the Karachi Press Club, one of the oldest and most prestigious organisations for journalists in Pakistan, I was granted permission to hold a press conference with the print media in total attendance. On 3rd December 2009, I held a press conference with my father, brother and uncle, giving me the courage and the boost I needed to face the media. I started by highlighting the lack of physical infrastructure, absence of any educational and livelihood opportunities for the disabled, lack of barrier-free access, the environment, and the attitudes of the society, none of which are conducive for the disabled. After presenting the current situation, I asked the media, *"what are we doing to reverse the situation? Do we have a plan of action as a civil society? What's the point of celebrating 3rd December if you aren't doing anything about it except making the same fake promises year after year?"*.

The press conference was the start of a new awareness in my life. I had changed course from being a victim to being a voice for all disabled, who I could see were victims of rampant injustices and, to a vast extent, ignorance in our society. People would bully us from using elevators as well. Can you imagine I had to wait to use an elevator, whereas people who could simply use an escalator would be trying to bypass me to get in the elevator? I consider myself an ambassador for disabled people. It can be taken as my first endeavour in the journey of activism for the rights of the disabled in Pakistan. The press conference gave me confidence and set the course for this new direction in my life.

I created a social group called *"Enable Pakistan"*, with 10 members from my close family and friends, with each member making some monetary contribution. Our first course of action was to gather data about the understanding of common people toward disability and the needs of the disabled. We did it through a survey by a group of volunteer college students. This survey data helped us understand the mindset and the lack of knowledge amongst common people towards disability. It made us realise that, if people don't even know about ramps, how would they know about the other problems we, the disabled, face? Considering the data collected, we decided to start with creating barrier-free access around a busy shopping centre in Karachi. The first step was building ramps for wheelchair users. The members pooled money for the materials, and the student volunteers did the labour work on a weekend.

While we were in the process of building these ramps, a small crowd of shopkeepers had gathered; they appreciated our efforts and asked questions, so we took this as an opportunity to enlighten them on the purpose of these ramps. They, in turn, told us that Karachi Metropolitan Corporation does not allow us to build ramps and came and broke ours, saying it's an encroachment. These shop vendors had earlier made ramps not for wheelchairs, but for their trollies. Two weeks later, we went and looked at the ramps, and there were literally carts/motorbikes passing over them; it was shocking!! We had worked so hard. This was another eyeopener on the lack of awareness. People did not have the slightest sense of why these ramps are essential for wheelchairs!!

This revelation made us understand as a small group that there is nothing much we could do to change the mindset of older people, so it made us think in the direction of informing the next generation. Our first step in this regard was to target schools. So, we started going to different schools, and the school kids came up with many interesting ideas about disability. A few said, *"this is God's curse on you"*; my answer to this question was, *"if this is God's curse, then how am I able to be in front of you. Don't you think maybe God put me in this position so that I would do something about it?"*. Our visits and these kinds of questions really helped us understand the young mindsets and from where these were being influenced. We could see how we could try and be instrumental in starting to change the young minds. Was I God's curse, or was I God's ambassador?

To carry this further, *Enable Pakistan* organised a speech competition on *'society's role in creating hurdles for the disabled,'* with participation from mainstream and some special schools in Karachi. A large multinational had kindly consented to be the sponsors of this event. The key objectives of mixing the able and disabled were to eliminate sympathy and charity from the non- disabled members of our society. We wanted to change the mindset of the non-disabled towards the disabled, as well as make some substantial changes and adjustments in the behaviour, attitudes and the services being provided for the disabled in Pakistan. Also invited were civil organisations, which included architects, builders and developers from the construction industry. These people were honest in accepting that they had no knowledge about barrier-free access and how it plays a vital role in providing services for the disabled. Barrier-free access involves the provision of alternative means of access to steps, e.g., ramps and elevators, for those with mobility problems. In Pakistan, there is no enforced law from the government instructing the local councils or municipalities to lay down the conditions of barrier-free access when constructing new buildings.

Through our various endeavours we continued to create awareness about disabilities and the rights of the disabled around the city of Karachi. We had to go to many educational institutions and organisations to do this, and most of them had no ramps or accessibility for wheelchair users.

In Pakistan, the disabled-friendly washrooms are designed for the elderly with some extra handles, but they have no awareness about the toilet needs for wheelchair users and other physical disabilities. Toilet facilities for a person with paraplegia have a different meaning; we need a commode chair, which you must shift onto and then be on the commode. After that, you must lie on the bed, change, sit on the chair, and move to the wheelchair. So, when I go out, it's very difficult for me if the toilet does not have these facilities or at least it is not large enough. Over time, I started researching and bought a folding commode chair and a folding wheelchair from abroad, and I carry them when I am travelling, even for a night. In the beginning, when I did not have these chairs, I couldn't even think about travelling without my brother, because he did all the shifting and the transfers that I needed.

A few years had passed since my accident, and I continued to apply for jobs, but could not land any employment. It was 2013, and I got an *Azm e Alishaan Award – Azm-e-Alishan* (the Glorious Resolve), which is a national awareness drive launched in Pakistan, initiated by concerned Pakistanis to enlighten and inspire the people for a better and progressive Pakistan, to re-create the spirit of nationhood for a positive future. The awards are given to honour Pakistanis worldwide whose everyday work helps show an accurate picture of a nation's spirit and potential. I received this award in recognition of my work in creating awareness about people in Pakistan with disabilities and helping them overcome them.

From 2003 at the time of my accident, till 2013, I did my bachelor's degree as well as my Master's and continued my activism, but I was still jobless and struggling to get some financial and emotional independence, where I could face the world on my own. I firmly believe that, if a person has a disability, it is very important for them to be financially and emotionally strong to lessen the insecurities and not burden their family or society. I realised how difficult it was to change society's mindset. Just because I was in a wheelchair, I was considered brain dead, so I shouldn't be given any opportunity. Owing to this frustration in 2015, I decided to leave Pakistan.

My Mamu passed away. He was a father figure to me, a pillar of strength and support. After my father, he was the one I would always turn to. With his death, my life was in tatters. Earlier, my brother got married. I was excited to welcome a new member to the family, yet I felt insecure. I thought the time, energy and emotional support he gave me throughout these years would now go to his wife and kids. I would be considered a burden, or so I thought.

I had to leave the country now and find life somewhere else. I had carefully thought about this, rationalised it, and decided to try my luck in a country that is more welcoming for the disabled and explore business and work opportunities.

I had been abroad many times before and after my accident, but it was always with family, with my brother being the most important support. I mustered up the courage and applied for a visit visa to the UK and, luckily, was granted one. My mother was my biggest support and always a tower of strength, but she was not happy with my decision, whereas my father was willing to accompany me on this exploratory trip.

As luck would have it, the evening before I left for the UK, I got a call for an interview from the Human Resource Manager at a multinational in Pakistan, who were the sponsors of a speech competition, arranged by *Enable Pakistan*. They had spotted me and were keen to give opportunities to the disabled in their organisation. Hearing this news, my mother was jubilant and insisted that I should cancel my trip. I explained to her how impossible it was to change my ticket. I called the HR manager and shared with them my plans and promised to get in touch once I got back from the UK.

Years had passed since my bachelor's, degree and by 2015 the rules and regulations had changed and were now not favourable for foreign job applicants. My father and I looked at an alternative option of a start-up business, but this wouldn't work, so we returned home after a good break of four months together. Looking back in hindsight, I firmly believe my mother's prayers brought me back to Pakistan.

The opportunity at the multinational was still open after my return. I passed the interview, cleared the test taken to ascertain my needs, and was hired as an intern. I again faced the dilemma of accepting the job or refusing it. Still, I again reminded myself of being the ambassador of the disabled and accepted the internship. I was a 32-year-old intern where my peers were 15 years younger than me. Despite the joy of getting the job, the realisation that life had pushed me back 15 years was equally traumatic.

I can tell you the generation gap was real. I was too old to socialise with my peers and much junior in the company to socialise with colleagues of my age group. On top of that, I was the punishment God had shown to the world, a person in a wheelchair. I used to eat alone at work during my lunch break. They liked my work during the two-month internship, so they hired me on a 6-months contract and after that I was hired on a permanent basis. My supervisor was to play a huge role in what I am today.

The organisation I worked for was housed in one of the few disabled-friendly modern offices in Karachi with ramps and elevators. The main thing that was missing was that there were no adequate toilet facilities for disabled people who are paraplegic and need a large washroom with space for changing. In the absence of a good washroom, despite repeated requests, I could not use the washroom during the office hours. I could not change my diaper, which I wear for my incontinence and is regularly issued to paraplegics. To manage this situation, I did not eat or drink during my office hours so as not to need to go to the washroom. Yet still, I had to face a long commute home. Many colleagues, especially the male ones did not understand my situation of not being able to eat or drink for the whole working day. So, it hurt when I heard nasty comments, *"Oh, you are leaving early, are you taking a half-day?"*. They did not realise or understand my challenges.

At first, I used to respond very politely to their ignorance, but I reached a stage where I challenged them to sit on a wheelchair the whole day, not eat or drink or not use the washroom and then, see who would leave early for home. I also wanted to remind them how during Ramadan when they were fasting, energy levels were low and they lacked concentration, the office hours were officially cut short, so that people could go home early. I told them that I was fasting, not 30 days in Ramadan, but 5 days a week, Monday to Friday during office hours. These were just my inner thoughts, and at the same time, I avoided being vocal about my problems and challenges. Work ethics and accountability are very important to me, so even if I left work at 5pm and there was some work pending, I would take the files home with me, usually to deal with on my long car journey home. I never wanted to give the impression that disabled people are lazy, weak and not hard working.

Besides it causing me a major health issue, not eating or drinking hindered my social inclusion at work. I felt left out as I could not enjoy the simple pleasures of sitting back, relaxing and enjoying a cup of tea with my colleagues during breaks. Colleagues could not understand why I did not accept offers to share a drink and snacks or go out with them during the lunch break. The places they went to were usually not wheelchair accessible, so even if I was occasionally invited, I politely refused, as it created too much hassle for my colleagues. Unsurprisingly, I do not get invited anymore. When we had our company get-togethers and dinners, sometimes people remembered that it must be accessible for Uzma, and sometimes they also forgot. I was disposable.

With time, the company started to give me opportunities. I was on a learning curve, as were they, teaching each other something new daily. I was afterwards also sent to Lahore University of Management Sciences (LUMS) for a course. When they were planning to send me, they learned that there were no ramps at LUMS and told the management that one of their employees was a wheelchair user and would require a ramp. The management built a ramp for that course and the next time I visited LUMS, one of the professors said to me, *"remember we built this ramp for you, and now others are using it"*. A change in the mindset? We can say that I was the change agent in this scenario, and I took it as an achievement.

Despite my disability, I was allowed, on an official trip to visit Sukkur, another major city in Pakistan. This was my first trip alone, without my family, and my first feeling of independence. When we landed at Sukkur airport, we realised that the airport did not have an ambilift, which is used as a boarding vehicle for disabled passengers, passengers with reduced mobility or mainly people using wheelchairs. Besides the ambilift, they did not have any facilities for the disabled. Whilst there are major industries in this city, like the rest of the country, nobody pays heed to the needs of the disabled, because I guess we are not even counted as part of the workforce?

To my astonishment and fear, four people held my wheelchair and brought me down the normal staircase of the plane. This event left me more frustrated and disappointed as I firmly believed that these are basic provisions that should be available for the disabled. Another setback after this event was as a caution the organisation would not send me on an official trip for the reasons of health and safety expense, as I would need a bulkhead seat, disabled-friendly toilet, and ambilifts.

My specialisation was in software engineering, but my permanent position was in the human resource department. I was conscious of this shortcoming and wanted to make the most of this opportunity that had come my way, so I undertook a one-year diploma in human resource management, which was part of an executive MBA - 2-year programme, offered by the prestigious Karachi Institute of Business Administration. I took this up as a challenge and had to shuffle between work, studies and home. It was very difficult, but I managed and got my post-graduate diploma in human resource management and secured second place and a silver medal. My managers were happy with my work. I felt blessed that I was financially independent, but I kept thinking, why can't I be promoted like my non-disabled peers? I wondered why I wasn't given opportunities like my colleagues. In my dreams, I wanted a world where these things were equal, because it seemed I had to constantly prove myself. I would ask myself, *"Why can't they see that I have worth? Why is my work always measured against my disability?"*.

I felt proud when I was asked to represent Pakistan at a Dubai international human resource conference. Pakistan is a nation gradually promoting and accepting the rights of the disabled. A decade ago, there was a glass ceiling for professional women. They never got promoted easily and were paid less than their male colleagues. With a united front, women have tried to shift the barrier, with a slight shift now in place. Today, the same glass ceiling is being applied to people with disabilities, who now face a barrage of challenges. We get hired and try to give our 100%, but we cannot change the mindset of employers and their insecurities. They have a lingering issue that when given a task, will the disabled be able to deliver? I know a united effort is being made to create awareness, and advocating this issue is much better. However, what will make a true difference, is to get the right and sincere people involved.

In Pakistan, there are now laws on barrier-free access in the government's national plan of action, but there is no enforcement; organisations are not even aware of these laws. Opportunities are there, but the infrastructure needs to be modified, if we want disabled people to have a role as valued citizens of the country. I am in touch with people with disabilities and we share our experiences guiding each other on social media platforms. For me, the workplace I dream of has barrier-free access with ramps, elevators, toilet facilities and staff rooms, where all the employees can go during their breaks. In addition to making the physical environment accessible, there is the issue of equal educational and employment opportunities. What the recent pandemic has taught us is that much work can be done from home. So, in the future, companies should allow work to be done from home a few days a week, where disabled people can also benefit.

My life was on track, kind of and there was some light at the end of the tunnel. Back home, however, my mother was dying inside. In Pakistani culture, a daughter's marriage is considered a sacred right of parents, a responsibility which, if delivered, brings honour to the family. I was 36 years old and had never received any marriage proposals, and neither did I expect any. This was eating up my mother; the *"sin"* of the mother and the daughter was playing on her mind.

In the beginning, when I was trying to come to terms with my disability, I tried to understand the culture in my country and the society's mindset toward disability. By choice, I did not want to be in any relationship, because it was in my mind that I must do something for society. My mother wanted to see me settled just like any other mother would wish for her daughter, but the reality was different for me, and I had come to terms with it. I knew I must be financially and emotionally independent to move forward with my disability. Emotionally I was very strong as Allah surrounded me with some great people, like my ever-supporting family and my dear uncle. If I saw the bad side of anyone, I would also see the good side; all this immensely helped my self- confidence and my self-esteem.

If you are a wheelchair user, in our culture, it is tough for a mother to accept a daughter-in-law in such a condition. Daughters-in-law are to serve the family and the household, not to be taken care of. I needed a lot of care and medically it cost a lot. I would probably never have children. Given my situation, I did not know if I could feel the need to marry or if I could ever complete a man's needs. I was marital suicide!

I met Maxud in 2014 when we did some social work together. I never realised he would discuss the topic of marriage with me. I was not sure of his intentions; people in my condition doubt everything that comes our way. Even though I had regained my confidence, I would still question the person willing to marry me. What are his reasons? *"Does he want to go to heaven? Gain airmiles with God?"*. So I told him frankly, *"I don't want you to go to heaven".*

As it is, marriage is a huge undertaking; in my case, it was a huge responsibility. I was in doubt, and I wasn't ready. On the other hand, he also matched my resilience, did not give up despite my refusal and came back with the proposal in 2017 again after 3 years of being in touch with me all the time.

My family started to second guess him. Was he a saint or the devil? Did he have any ulterior motives? Of course, we did believe true love exists and also realised the seriousness of his proposal when it came a second time. Very openly, my parents explained to him all the challenges that a person with paraplegia can have for the rest of their life, and the possibility of my inability to conceive and bear a child. After considering this, Maxud boldly decided to opt for love and left the rest to destiny.

My family's intervention was realistic and showed how much they cared about me and my happiness. My father was reluctant. My brother counselled my father, *"What is the worst that can happen? Will she get divorced? And come back to live with us? She is already living with us for all these years; if this gives her one chance to taste life, even if it is for 01 days, we need to give her that chance".*

Against all odds, I got married in 2018. My mother was no more a sinner. Her daughter had gotten married. It was a very joyous occasion for my family and me. At the same time, I had mixed feelings, as I was from a family which had totally accepted my disability in every way; my every wish was granted however possible. I was entering an unknown world that was bound to carry some apprehensions. Apart from that I felt happy and enjoyed every moment of the celebrations.

Culturally, Pakistani weddings have celebrations for weeks before the wedding day. We tried to limit it to three events: *mehndi, baraat* and the *valima*, with not too much spending on unnecessary things. The first event of *mehndi* (the henna ceremony) is where the bride applies henna in intricate designs on her hands and feet, and female family and friends do the same with lots of singing wedding songs and dancing. All my family, relatives and friends who attended wanted to share their joy at my happiness.

On my *baraat* (wedding) day, I was brought to the event in a buggy. I was transferred from the car to the cart, and the same cart became the wedding stage. On my *valima* (bridegroom's side dinner), we made sure that we got to the venue early before the arrival of guests to get settled on the stage. Both times it was done to avoid becoming an unnecessary spectacle in transferring from the wheelchair. I dislike extravagance, so I was mindful of limiting unnecessary expenses at all three events.

Relatives and friends expressed different opinions when they heard about my marriage. Well, you can say it was a surprise for everyone that a disabled wheelchair user is tying the knot with a non-disabled person.

As for Maxud side, he never shared any negative comments, even if there were any. I get asked repeatedly over the years: what made him choose you as a life partner and how he managed to convince his family. To the first one, his response has always been, *"I like your qualities, you are honest, you never give up on things, you accepted the challenge of life".* He doesn't talk about the convincing part; he must have done it with difficulty, but if he chooses not to repeat now, then I respect his silence.

Luckily, we are on the ground floor, and before we got married, my husband, to suit my needs, had a ramp made at the entrance for my wheelchair and modified the washroom. He is very nice, yes, Masha Allah (Allah protect us); he is very cooperative and understanding towards my needs and desires, and I try and reciprocate.

Since my marriage, I have had a renewed self-confidence and energy, allowing me to take a bold step in changing my job and following a career in HR. I am now an HR specialist in another multinational, where I am given work on merit, and there are adequate toilet facilities on the same floor. However, because of my disability, life is a constant battle, and I see myself at the forefront of change. What I have now could not have been imagined fifteen years ago. It is a paradigm shift, and I remain confident that other disabled women will get equal opportunities, and in the coming years, there will be a shift in society in the needs of the disabled.

Today looking back, if I was given a pen and paper by destiny to write down for myself whatever I want in life, I would get it. Had I written it down alone, I would have missed out on a thousand bounties that I already have in life. I can enjoy ice cream, I share a cup of tea with my husband, I play with my niece and nephew as if they are my own children, I can hug my parents, I can buy anything I like without asking anyone, I have a sense of gratitude.

The writer of destiny has written for me what I could not even imagine for myself. When I was living, I was only thinking about myself. When my journey started, I realised that life is not about us, but about others. I may have sinned. I may have been punished. But through me, God has opened the doors for many people's repentance and blessings, people who I pray for every night, people who understood me, helped me and took away my pain from me.

What I am today could not be possible without my father and his enormous support in everything that I did, and my younger sister Maria, who woke up in the middle of many nights to cater for my needs. Verily, waking in the middle of the night to pray to Allah is one of the superior forms of worship in our religion. Waking in the middle of the night to help a needy person is one of the most selfless acts one can do. I must say, one door shuts, ten more open. We must wait for destiny to take us where we belong. In CS Lewis's words, *Onwards and upwards*...I can say the journey so far has been far from pity to WOW!

Zarina's story

There was a lot that I had to prove to myself and to others. I had to take hold of the narrative and turn it on its head! I had to be my own person, and I had to fight for that right...

I didn't want the pity or the sympathy; I didn't want any crutches for myself in any form. I wanted to be independent and self-reliant, and then any beautiful bond that came my way, I could take that, accept it and embrace it as an added blessing

I am Zarina Hasan, and my story began on 17th November 1973 in Peshawar, Pakistan. Peshawar is the capital city of the Pakistani province of Khyber Pakhtunkhwa and is the sixth-largest city in Pakistan. My father was a chartered accountant, my mother a housewife, and I have a younger sister. Peshawar was a small city then, where everybody knew everybody. My childhood was happy, and I was surrounded by family, friends, and my pets. Since my childhood, I have been in love with nature and preferred being outdoors and had to be dragged indoors when it got dark. I remember playing in the garden, studying in it, especially in the winter sunshine, and I would doze off, wake up with a jolt and realise there was a book I had not studied.

Our house was a mini zoo with pets, including birds, cats, dogs, sheep, goats, turkeys, quails, and pheasants. I loved pets, and before going to school, I would make sure that all of them were well looked after. Coming home, the first thing I did was to attend to them. Any pet lover would know about the heartbreak that goes together with the joy, and it was such a special bond, my pets and me!

I had these hand-reared fluffy chicks, the ones you get from the farm. One would like to nestle at the nape of my neck, and the other would want to sleep on my chest. I remember I would just lay still and not move a muscle; I would not even yield to the temptation of going to the toilet or anything so they wouldn't be disturbed. At one point, I had six cats who competed for my attention. The big ones would fling the little ones off my lap, and the kittens would sprawl all over the furniture. The cats had their personalities; one cat would want to be inside the quilt, and another would feel claustrophobic and want to be outside. My sister and I shared a room with twin-connected beds, and she used to have this line drawn on the bedclothes with the threat, *"if a cat dares to cross over to my side, you won't have your plat in the morning".*

Besides my pets, my childhood was also rich and exciting, with my friends close to me. Since the age of three, there was a clutch of us, and when we made our career choice, we all opted for medicine, went to the same medical college and are still the best of friends today. My father was a professional self-made man who always supported and encouraged me in whatever I chose to do. We had a very loving relationship and a very close bond. He was very hard-working, possessed a strong will, and conducted himself with dignity, despite for a long time having severe health issues. My parents brought us up with a defined and absolute sense of right and wrong, and in our home, there were always reasons, but no excuses.

Growing up, my thoughts constantly changed on choosing a career: becoming a zoologist, marine biologist, or a doctor. Despite my father being against me becoming a medical doctor, I still chose medicine. Maybe, my decision at a subconscious level was influenced by his long-term illness. In the early '90s, I started my course in medicine, and by 1997, I graduated and became a doctor. A year later, I completed a year-long internship in internal medicine and surgery.

I wanted to specialise in genetics, so I explored worldwide options. Genetics is a branch of biology concerned with studying genes, genetic variation, and heredity in organisms. Imperial College London, UK, offered a Master's course in Molecular Virology and Pathology of Viruses, and I felt that was right up my street. This M.Sc. was to be a bridge between the world of clinical medicine and a laboratory - based career. I enjoyed my Master's and completed it in 2000. As a step further, I applied and got accepted onto the PhD programme at the University of Manchester Institute of Science and Technology (UMIST).

My father, as mentioned, had been quite sick, and his concern was that a PhD would take a few years, between 3-5, and he felt he didn't have a lot of time to live and wanted me to be settled and near him. I had worked hard during my Master's and was passionate about getting a PhD. It was a tough decision to let go of my dream of getting a doctorate. My friends and 'batchmates' pleaded and argued with me to take back my decision, but I sacrificed happily for my father, as he was very precious to me.

After my MSc, I returned to Pakistan, married in 2001 and settled in Karachi. At the beginning of 2002, I joined Aga Khan University of Health Sciences (AKUH) as a faculty member. I applied for a PhD programme in Health Sciences and got a full scholarship for two years. I was working at AKUH as a lecturer in molecular biology, a researcher and a PhD student and enjoying the challenge. My first son was born at the end of 2002, and my focus was mainly on raising my son and managing a healthy work/home balance.

In 2003, my firstborn, who was just eight months, fell very ill with Rotavirus. The virus usually causes fatal gastroenteritis, so there is severe vomiting and diarrhea. After being diagnosed, within a week, his weight plummeted, so, I put everything on hold and could not continue with my work at AKUH. My focus was on getting my son's immunity to kick back and become a healthy, robust child. In between, I would come across projects and in 2004, I wrote up a significant grant proposal to the World Health Organisation (WHO) for setting up an Influenza Surveillance Programme in Pakistan. The same year my father fell very ill, so I moved back to Islamabad for about 18 months to care for and be near him. I was there with him when he passed away. To this day, I miss him! He's left a void in my life that no one can fill; he and I had this amazingly unique rapport, and he was a true friend!

After my father passed away, I moved to Karachi and was advised that a grant application proposal I had previously written, had come through. I became the first female virologist in Pakistan and was selected to head a programme that was a collaboration between the National Institute of Health and the World Health Organization. As my family comes first, I declined the offer as the position was based in Islamabad, and we, at the time, were settled in Karachi. The project was a success, and as a result of a surveillance programme the National Institute of Health had initiated, Pakistan was able to control and eradicate Bird Flu when it broke out in 2008.

In 2009, I had my second son and in 2010, when he was about a year old, I felt that since my firstborn was sturdy and the younger one was a healthy baby, I could go back full-time to my career. I thought I could balance my work and home life, but there was another unexpected turn. My first born, now 8 years old, was excited to do an experiment he had learnt in school. The experiment was that, if you cover one eye and focus on an object through the other eye, the eye perceives that object to move and slightly shift.

How many of us walk around covering an eye? We invariably use both eyes. When I covered my right eye, I could not see anything with my left eye. That is when I went rushing to the eye clinics. I couldn't read the eye chart with the left eye. When my eye pressure was measured, it clocked in a 50 rather than 15, which is considered normal. There was panic amongst the practitioners; they all had the same question: *"what happened?"*. There were many diagnoses. Some saw it as a possible tumour; someone was focusing on optic neuritis, and another had multiple sclerosis in mind. All these diagnoses were being dished out one after the other, as if somebody were reading the day's news to me. It was discovered that I had lost sight in one eye because of glaucoma!

Glaucoma is a common eye condition where the optic nerve, which connects the eye to the brain, becomes damaged. It's usually caused by fluid building up in the front part of the eye, which increases pressure inside the eye. Glaucoma can lead to a loss of vision, if it's not diagnosed and treated early. It's a bit of a mystery, I don't know exactly when it happened, but when I discovered it, I had already lost sight in one eye.

I have had been highly myopic since the age of twelve. Short-sightedness, or myopia, is a common eye condition that causes distant objects to appear blurred, while close things can be seen clearly. Being myopic, every six months, I was continuously monitored for any complications and never missed my ophthalmology appointments.

Being near-sighted, one is at risk of retinal detachments and retinal tears, so it wasn't any negligence on my part. There are two types of glaucoma, open-angle, and closed-angle. I have open-angle glaucoma when the eye produces more fluid than its ability to drain and pump liquid out of it. In a closed angle, there is an obstruction to any outflow, which results in increased pressure on the eye. In my case, as it happens at an open angle, there is no pain, redness or tearing; hence there are no alarming symptoms as such, but secretly the pressure was high and damaging the nerve. Given my six-month check-ups, I don't know why this wasn't detected. It later came to light that my glaucoma developed, and the nerve-damaged must have started when I was in medical college even though I had proper and regular check-ups!

Being a doctor, I asked many questions during the investigations on my eye and the medications I was prescribed. I was expecting my third and youngest son in the same year. The doctors did not consider the stress or the psychological effect I was under, but to my amazement and horror, being a medical doctor and asking questions was held against me. It was not as if the medical professionals did not know what was happening to my eye; I think they just refused to accept what was staring them in the face. I think they were looking for a more exotic reason for my problem, rather than the obvious one. Consequently, time was wasted on medications, and there was no sense of urgency that should have been there, as I had a very rare and aggressive form of the disease. The question of medical ethics crossed my mind from time to time, but I put all this down to experience and learned from it.

2010 was the turning point in my life, for when the diagnosis came through, I realised I had lost sight in one eye. Dealing with this reality, trying to overcome the shock, and hearing the disbelief of the professionals and practitioners, did not help me. It hadn't dawned on them how their behaviour affected me as a patient and made me anxious. It was a tough time as I was also nursing my year-old middle son and had to drag him around the hospital waiting rooms and clinics for hours and hours on an end.

I was advised to have surgery on the eye with the lost vision and needed trabeculectomy surgery. This is when a hole is dug into the eyeball through the trabecular meshwork, the eye's drainage system. It is an invasive process, and although it is standard surgery for glaucoma, because I was pregnant and every organ behaves differently during this period, no one was willing to operate on me. I chose to have the operation in Singapore because of their advanced medical expertise in ophthalmology. I am the only case to date; before me, my surgeon had not come across a case where he had to operate an invasive procedure on a pregnant patient. There was a sharp contrast in medical care between the two countries. In Singapore, my surgeon's first statement was, *"you, concentrate on your pregnancy and carrying your baby to be as healthy as can be, and I will take care of what needs to be taken care of"*. This is how medicine should be.

During surgery, I refused sedation because I was eight months pregnant, and there was no foetal monitoring in the operating theatre. There was a risk that the baby would fall asleep with the effect of the sedative. Throughout the pregnancy, I had repeated ultrasounds and was scared of malformations. At seven months of my pregnancy, I was advised to choose between the eye or carrying the pregnancy through to term. I'm a firm believer in the gift of life! I felt this love and affection for my unborn child, so this was never a question for me, and the alternative was never an issue.

Following my decision to keep my baby, there was anger and disapproval in the family. Even to this day, I'm very careful to shield my youngest against careless, irresponsible comments like, *"oh, so this is the child who cost you, your eye"*. It was traumatic and difficult, but he was, the most perfect little baby born in February 2011. He is the only one amongst my three who was bottle-fed and not nursed.

Singapore has always pulled me away from the brink regarding damage control. Knowing that I had just undergone surgery, I had to fly back and forth between Singapore and Karachi for follow-ups, taking out stitches, etc. I hired nurses to care for my youngest as I made a conscious decision not to have my baby bond with me emotionally till 3-6 months, when the gap between the follow-ups would be long enough for him not to suffer separation and anxiety from being away from me. It was also misinterpreted as a lack of love and care on my part, which I find so ludicrous, especially given the sort of choices and decisions I made out of love. I was expected to prove or explain myself to people when it was none of their business. I was being judged every step of the way, whether financial, medical or grieving for a loved one. There was so much I was dealing with, and on top of that, uncalled pressure piled up. There were times when I was in so much denial and despair that I wanted to scream and shout to show my anger.

Initially, when the problem with my eye happened, I was looking for support everywhere, especially support from my family when something like this happens. My family was supportive, and it was certainly helpful, but at times their stifling overprotectiveness was suffocating. It is sometimes hard for people to understand where you are coming from and your needs.

Suddenly, I couldn't understand anything anymore. I couldn't understand myself, let alone others. There was a lot of anger and denial – it was like being caught in a tornado or a shipwreck being tossed and rolled from one end to the other; I had hit rock bottom, and at that point, I had to hold on to something and move on. It was a decision I had to make. Healing doesn't begin until acceptance comes in; it is also an individualised and personalised journey. I had to go through a state of complete breakdown to recover and then decide what I needed to do to pull myself out of this and not succumb to the negativity that I felt surrounded me.

The start of 2012 was a very stressful time for my family. My husband's business suffered, and we faced bankruptcy, another added stress. I was not processing my emotions very well either; I had zero self-esteem; I would react in a certain way or make entirely disastrously wrong judgements. There were volatile tempers; the children were growing up; the youngest was one, the middle was three and the eldest was nine. In short, it was a turbulent time, so the decision to move to Islamabad was based on giving ourselves some breathing space and bringing some normality into our lives. At that time, my husband did not see eye to eye with me, but now he understands and appreciates that it was for the best.

Islamabad, the capital of Pakistan, is a relatively quieter city than Metropolitan Karachi. Slowly, everything began falling into place because everybody had room and space. I decided to live on my own with my children and not with my mother, who lived in Islamabad. Even at that stage, I was not allowed to show despair, hopelessness, anger – nothing. Even in that state of mind, I was expected to grin, smile and be on my best behaviour, which is too much to ask of anyone.

Six months after moving to Islamabad, I started working at the National Agricultural Research Centre (NARC). The project was on zoonosis, which is a disease that is passed on from animals to humans. It was a US-based project in collaboration with the Centre for Disease Control in Atlanta. This was the first time a project was executed under the *'the one-health umbrella'*, where medics and veterinarians would join hands and work together. I was the medic on board with a team of veterinarians, and I was heading my lab. I was selected for the above project on merit. The board, the director, and the panel knew I only had one eye functioning. With one eye, you lose perception in depth, and I had made it clear from the beginning that I would require assistance when it came to certain procedures or readings. My salary and job covered a small fraction of my expenses, but I had my assets to fall back on. The job was more of a token of defiance and my independence and rebellion, kept me sane. I had an understanding team that flexed and bent the rules for me.

My surgeon in Singapore had predicted that my second eye would be affected after five years. In the meantime, monitoring the eye was the only option. For five years, the eye showed no signs of being affected, then like clockwork, I started to experience signs of losing my sight. Whilst it was tough, as a pragmatic person, I had prepared myself for what could come. So, before losing sight in the second eye, I started doing research and got hold of a white cane and a braille box. I started teaching myself to be mobile. People around me thought I was despairing, lacking faith, and all the time, I kept hearing, *"You are being despondent, you do not have faith, your vision will be restored in the affected eye, and you will not lose sight in the second eye".* Even when I reached out for rehabilitation, it was met with negative comments. Rather than scrambling around when the sky fell on top of me with a thud, I wanted to be prepared, and I'm glad I made these decisions. Many times, I felt as if I had developed a split personality. On the one hand, I was struggling to do whatever I could to slow the progression of the disease, whereas, on the other hand, Singapore's goal was to prepare me for it, which I totally agreed with. Amidst all, I am not denying that I didn't have negative thoughts; I even had suicidal thoughts.

My kids also showed signs of anxiety; the middle one had a speech delay. All the things that a mother does instinctively, I had to stop doing, like picking up the kids, cuddling them, and they had to adapt to these changes. I was not allowed to lift weights, so these toddlers had to learn to sit on their mother's knee. It was challenging to restrain myself and curtail the instinct and impulse to scoop my children into my arms.

My vision was being affected, and I lost a line on the Snellen chart every week. A Snellen chart is an eye chart that can measure visual acuity. The chart is named after the Dutch ophthalmologist Herman Snellen. In glaucoma, the sight you lose does not come back; it's irreversible! For me, every week, to have a line wiped out from that chart, I cannot begin to describe the panic that I felt; I was drowning! I knew this, but when it happened, I didn't want it to happen, and it was a very rapid decline. I didn't have a third eye to fall back on. Despite every effort, I lost sight of that eye within months. That was a totally different traumatising experience.

In a way, once I lost that eye, the surgeries came to a grinding halt; that was a big relief because there is a three-month recovery period with many restrictions between surgeries. Each time there was a surgery, I had to be absent from my home, leaving the children behind, who were very young. I had to wear an eye shield for protection, even when sleeping. I couldn't rub my eye, so when the surgeries were finished, and nothing else could be done, it gave me time to focus on my children and home; it came as a blessing.

The biggest relief was the disappearance of the terrible floaters that would be dancing before my eyes when I had one eye that functioned. When sight went from both eyes, the floaters obviously went away. Floaters are black dots or shiny showers of light, black threads, or worms constantly moving about in your field of vision. 'The finish' was in Singapore, where I had my last surgery in 2015.

The loss of my sight was something I knew all along, but in Pakistan I was pushed to deny it. However, when I heard in Singapore, that I would completely lose my sight, it came like a punch in the stomach. Sometimes you don't want to listen to what you already know — sometimes, you want to be proved wrong. I had a good cry, and that was it. On the other hand, it did help put me back on track.
This was 2016; I buckled down and just dealt with it.

The counsellor in Singapore I had sessions with had also lost her sight in her 20s. She holds a degree in

Psychology from an Australian University and applauded me for not feeling ashamed to use my white cane. Once I had accepted the reality, I didn't sound crazy to myself anymore. Whatever fears, apprehensions, plans, or hopes I had, I could share them with somebody who had been through that situation. Observing her being okay, being a professional, and carrying on with her life having lost her sight, and with a child with good sight, gave me immense comfort and support, which I cannot put into words. I also understood through counselling that asking for help and assistance when needed is okay. I sought advice on eating, dressing, shopping, organising my home, walking, listening to sounds, etc. It was as if I had been dropped into the sea and had to learn to swim and survive. I was lost, and it had to be a rebirth: the end of one life and the start of another.

It's not easy to adjust and accept, especially when seeing another side to life. It's not to say that your trials are harder than anybody else's, but if somebody has never experienced sight, they would have never known what 'sight' loss is and cannot really feel the loss of it as opposed to if you lose it in your mid 30s or early 40s. It's totally a different ball game. At this point, I started to view my loss of sight as a gift and learned to overcome my biggest fear, blindness. I paused, reflected, and now I am very much at peace.

I resigned from my job after I lost my second eye. There was a lot that I had to prove to myself and to others. I had to take hold of the narrative and turn it on its head! I had to be my own person, and I had to fight for that right. There were so many things that I had taken for granted till that time. I also had to create a closure around me to attain some semblance of acceptance and setting boundaries. It was now a different set of dynamics in play as to the person I was perceived to be and who silently I had evolved into. I had to come to terms with myself and make others understand, and if not understand, then simply accept.

I didn't want the pity or the sympathy; I didn't want any crutches for myself in any form. I wanted to be independent and self-reliant, and then any beautiful bond that came my way, I could take that, accept it and embrace it as an added blessing. I just flipped the lid – and from that point on, everything was just so beautiful – even though it was different. Once I accepted independence and self-reliance, I embraced it, learned to adapt to it and grew with it. It transformed me and changed my perception of the world around me, the people in it and me, and ever since, there has been no looking back.

Once I started living and organising my new life, the first thing I did was create a blog and called it, *Sight Beyond Sight*. I started writing because, at the time, I had not met anyone else who had either lost their vision or was losing their sight. In my first blog, *"Learning to Be Literate Again"*, I mentioned that, although I could not see what I write, my hand was programmed to process my thoughts. I pen down my thoughts, then type from memory using voice typing and touch typing using the software JAWS. I never learnt braille; probably, I didn't feel the need to. These days Smartphones come with their own speech recognition software depending on their operating systems. For reading my text, I use POLARIS, which has a talk-back option, and smartphones also have it.

Besides creating my own blog, I also paint. One day, I remember hiking in the hills, and I could hear the leaves and the birds – and felt the grass and the rocks. Suddenly, (I think it was a day in spring), I felt the sun's warmth, and I was basking in it, imagining the golden hue and the tint that the leaves and everything would have. That is when I felt the urge to somehow portray all of this. I drew and painted as a child and then, at college and university, but did so as assignments. I used to do a lot of colouring as a child; I was very good at shading and blending pencils, but I never painted or created anything original. I didn't even know what art material to use; I just turned up at a simple stationery store and asked for the basics of oil painting. I bought the smallest, cheapest, student-grade canvas, colours, basic brushes and oils.

In the beginning, I didn't even realise I had to work on the background of my paintings. I remember the first I did, and my children commented, *"it looks like Styrofoam because you have all these whites peeping through all the negative space, so how are you going to fill that in? you can't see?"*. Then, I realised I needed to work on the background. In no time, the children, my friends, and family were positive about my paintings, and some even wanted to hang them in their homes! This made me aware that I might be good at this.

I use my memory and imagination for my paintings. If I'm painting from memory, that memory will not stretch for months. So, if there is an unfinished piece, I have this urgency to get back to it asap and get it done in days. I like harmony in my paintings; if I am painting a rose, I will always want to carry the colours of the petals into the leaves. For me, the picture must bind and gel to be harmonious, and I like movement in my work; I do not go for still images that don't sing or speak.

I feel my work must be vibrant, have motion and soul, and be beyond realism. It has to say something, I want people to touch that *'rose'* or want to *'smell'* it or feel the *'breeze'*. If I paint waves, I want people to hear the *'crash'* the same way I hear them. For me, painting is part logic, part maths, but most of it is a feeling, an instinct and I trust my instincts. I use basic primary colours and arrange them in a specific sequence. This is where the logic comes in. Primary colours I use are blue, red and yellow, and then, I use a combination of the three; I have white and black on standby. Then I have an idea of what colour scheme I'm going for the shades I want.

So, if I want pink, I will use red and white – if I want to make a darker pink, there will be more red and less white or vice versa, if I wish to make it lighter. Or in watercolours, I will tone it down with water – in oils, I'll use more oil...
As to when or how I know it is done? It is done when I 'feel' it is done.

As to adding colours and bringing in shades, I think in the same way that I would know how much to walk from my front door to the gate – before stubbing my nose into the gate; it's a sense of distance, I suppose. I can't see the image, but again, the smartphone comes to the rescue; it usually describes an image. It won't say a daffodil. It will say a yellow flower, then I will connect the pieces of information or my children describe a thing to me and then, my imagination will take over. Sometimes, it makes me wonder what I create or paint! I ask my domestic staff; I ask my children, from a viewer's point of view, is it complete? Because sometimes I know it is done; sometimes an odd child will come and suggest that you need more details.

On the other hand, I have an idea where I wanted that painting to go, and I will say *"no"* this is what I want it to be. Sometimes, I'm painting, and my eldest will come and take the brush away from me, and he will say, *"you're done! stop right there!"*.

I am very moody and temperamental, and the weather plays a role in how I feel. If it's a pleasant, breezy, overcast day, then I love to be outdoors, and I love to hike. I was never athletic before losing sight, but when I moved to Islamabad in 2012, I was introduced to the hills and fell in love with them. Of course, I don't do it alone since losing my sight, and usually, I'm accompanied by either a friend or a staff member or sometimes by my children. Staying indoors makes me restless, and if I must be indoors, I will find a secluded corner, and I would prefer to write. I can paint with the chaos around me, but I can't write if there is chaos. So many images constantly dance around in my mind's eye. I have visualised ideas, themes, and concepts in my head that I want to transfer onto canvas.

Writing and breaking into art offered an outlet, a voice and something more productive and constructive to do. There was no large ambition behind these ventures; they were primarily forms of expression for me. The words I wrote or spoke or the images I created on canvas were being noticed, commanding attention; this is when I realised that this could work wonders. It could bridge the communication gap, and I could effectively share my thoughts and experiences through these mediums.

By this time, the conversation centered around 'my blindness'. I, a person, a professional, was not being acknowledged as a functioning human being, as I have been all my life. Any endeavour I tried or anything I accomplished was dismissed as something to occupy my mind or deflect attention from my disability.

Until I lost sight, I never really thought about visual impairment. After losing my sight, it got me thinking that, if I am going through this trauma with my privileged background, what happens to financially poor people and those who are emotionally not that strong. Many slip through the cracks and cannot pull themselves through. They are unwilling to adjust, adapt or accept the alternative it presents – it is a very serious issue, especially what happens to women.

So besides writing my blog, and painting, I also joined a vocational training institute for disabled and destitute women as a volunteer to understand how I could reach out to them and be more effective in providing help. Each woman was given training in their own group, and none of the group would interact with another disability group. The women I felt didn't have a sense of themselves even within that functional environment. Despite it being aimed at making them skilled enough to earn a living within the confines of their homes, the majority lacked confidence, and the ones that did shine and stand out were the ones who had been educated to primary, middle or graduate level. There were so many things that I began to understand while in that environment; the most important was the value of education. This asset had come to my rescue and became my strength, allowing me to make a life for myself when *I was written off* by society.

I realised that by having a voice and a presence through my blog and art, I could use it to create awareness about the importance of education for the disabled, especially women. Hence the birth of my organisation, *Sight Beyond Sight*, the aim of which is to create awareness that what may appear as a limitation, or a handicap is not necessarily the case. There is so much more to a person who is living with a disability than what meets the eye. My home is open to many, and then there is online access. I get myself to schools, offices or slums or to street schools or street children, wherever it doesn't matter. Counselling is also a component of the services I and my organisation offers.

My organisation did not come with premises and in

2019 I wrote up a grant proposal to have a resource centre to make printed matter accessible to visually challenged students and professionals. The idea was to get state-of-the-art technology to cater for the needs of visually challenged people, from electronic magnifiers to scanners, text to speech readers, braille embossers, printers and 3D printers.

I started floating the idea around in 2020; I engaged Microsoft, The National University of Sciences & Technology (NUST), an engineering school in Islamabad and then, the government. It attracted attention; the proposal was accepted and approved last year, and the tender opened and matured. Now it's in a two-stage implementation process.

Stage one will establish a resource centre at the National Library in Islamabad. Whereas the second phase will upgrade the Al Maktoum Special Education Centre – the blind school for boys and girls run by the government. The government has formed a number of committees and I am on the technical one overseeing its progress. With its funding, the project is under the government's control, and then later, it will be open for public-private partnerships. If Microsoft and NUST want to join, they will have the opportunity to do so. Losing my sight due to glaucoma has propelled me into creating glaucoma awareness. With my good and bad experiences along this journey, I feel I can do much to help make life better for others. This year I joined hands with two other visually impaired artists from the USA interested in showcasing their work to create glaucoma awareness.

The exhibition was very successful, and the painting I selected to be auctioned was sold for $1000.

My paintings are my source of livelihood, but I also use this for creating awareness and fundraising. Every year, I select some prints of my originals and design and produce merchandise based on them. The merchandise is then distributed and sold in batches. One year, I designed postcards, another year, I designed and sold greeting cards. Last year, I designed and sold tea coasters and mugs. After the first year, I had my first solo exhibition; since then, I have had a solo exhibition every year. It's not bad, considering that I started in 2017, and my paintings sell throughout the year.

I would like to see a more inclusive society, which doesn't just pat one another on the back. A society where there is awareness of special needs, where there is a responsibility to provide access, resources, and infrastructure for these diversities and where empathy replaces pity. A lot of work needs to be done regarding learning disabilities in schools. Real inclusion goes beyond sharing space physically. It calls for proper programming, a support system and trained teachers to implement it.

Owing to our campaigning, the parliament of Pakistan, with its houses of national assembly and senate, will open its doors to people with disabilities. We will have physical access as well as having us as board members. They plan to have some of my work on display in the assembly buildings. At least there is an engaging dialogue, which was not happening before.

I get emails, drafts and documents from everywhere, seeking my opinion as well as my other colleagues. All our recommendations and suggestions are valued and pooled together to try and narrow the gap between legislation and implementation.

Another issue I want to hammer home is medical ethics! The medical fraternity needs to change its attitude in handling diagnoses and how patients receive them. It must deliver news honestly and humanely. Being honest about not having the correct answers all the time or accepting their limitations, rather than just stubbornly dragging the patient emotionally, physically or financially to a place where the person finds it difficult to hold on to hope is not good.

Also, every year around the world, including in Pakistan, we celebrate the International Day of the Disabled, but we lose sight of the significance of this day, the struggle and the rights of the disabled and the awareness of the responsibilities that relentlessly carry-on day after day. We must take everybody along – as they say, no one should be left behind – as we propel ourselves forward, make changes, and achieve our goals!

So, there is a lot to be done, but I think we are moving in the right direction. The shift must also come from within the community of people living with a disability. We ought to change the notion of handouts; if this change, the body language changes, and ultimately the tone, the confidence, the self-worth – everything changes. People with a disability don't need the bar lowered on

their behalf; what they need to do is to step up to it and
raise it!